SEÁN LEMASS

A Biography

MICHAEL O' SULLIVAN

BLACKWATER PRESS

Printed in Ireland at the press of the publishers 1994

Editors
Olivia Hamilton
Anna O'Donovan

Design & Layout
Edward Callan

Cover
Gabrielle Stafford

ISBN   0 86121 583 4

© – Michael O' Sullivan 1994

Produced in Ireland by
Blackwater Press
c/o Folens Publishers
8 Broomhill Business Park,
Tallaght, Dublin 24.

For My Mother
And to the memory of my grandfather, David Slattery

CONTENTS

INTRODUCTION

'I am very perturbed by the information that you are thinking of writing my biography....When I am retired or dead will be quite time enough – if anybody is then likely to be interested'. That was Seán Lemass's reaction, in 1960, when he was informed that his biography was about to be written. He did not hinder in any way, the writer Liam Skinner, who was undertaking the task. However the work was never published. In 1962 he agreed to give a series of interviews to Risteárd Ó Glaisne who proposed a biography in Irish. That work suffered the same fate as Mr Skinner's. It is now eleven years since Professor Brian Farrell's biography of Lemass was first published.

In the writing of this book I have been extremely fortunate in having at my disposal, the private papers of Seán Lemass and the cooperation of his family. This help was offered without precondition.

This portrait of Lemass was compiled largely from those papers, from the cabinet papers, from interviews which Lemass gave to writers and journalists and from interviews with his family, friends and former colleagues.

I am especially grateful to Sean Lemass's grandson, Sean O'Connor, for introducing me to his parents, John and Sheila O'Connor who gave me every possible assistance with the book. John O'Connor guided me through a veritable sea of Lemass's private papers and photographs. Sheila O'Connor introduced me to her sisters, Maureen (Mrs Charles Haughey) and Peggy (Mrs Jack O'Brien) who gave me extensive interviews about their father.

I am extremely indebted to the former Taoiseach, Charles J. Haughey, for granting me a most extensive interview about his father-in-law. In this regard I also wish to thank Neil T. Blaney TD, former Senator Eoin Ryan and his son Eoin Ryan TD. I also wish to acknowledge the help give me by former political opponents of Sean Lemass.

Senator Maurice Manning and Edward Mulhall, Managing Editor RTE News, read the manuscript and I am obliged to them for their helpful suggestions.

Mr Barney Cavanagh of RTE gave me valuable information about Lemass's internment in Ballykinlar and I thank him for it. I had the benefit of the considerable assistance given me by Randal McDonnell of the Glens who gave generously of his time and advice. I had the encouragement of many friends chief amongst them, Mrs A. T. Keane who graciously gave her undivided support from the book's conception through to its final stages. My thanks also go to the Hon. Elizabeth Vereker, Mr Jerry Scanlan of RTE and the staff of the Oireachtas Library, the National Library, the library of University College Dublin and Trinity College Dublin, the National Archive and the John F. Kennedy Memorial Library.

Finally my thanks go to the people most closely involved with the production of the book: Olivia Hamilton and Anna O'Donovan for judicious editing and my publisher, John O'Connor for commissioning the book.

Michael O'Sullivan
Dublin 1994.

1

BOY SOLDIER

It is a curious but not totally unsustainable notion that so distant an historical event as the revocation of the Edict of Nantes by Louis XIV in 1685 might have had an influence on the making of modern Ireland. When the Protestant Henry of Navarre changed his religion to become king of France he had safeguarded the rights of his former co-religionists by signing that instrument in 1598. It guaranteed that the Protestant Huguenot minority would be allowed to exist in a largely Catholic country. When the edict was withdrawn all religious toleration of the Huguenots went with it. Many converted but over 200,000 fled. Some 50,000 escaped to England and about 10,000 made their way to Ireland. Some of those who lived in Ireland had first settled in England and in Scotland.

Amongst those who eventually made their home in Scotland was a family called le Maistre whose name with the passage of time became anglicised to Lemass. In Dublin the name in its original form of le Maistre is not recorded before the eighteenth century when it became well-known in city business circles. It disappears after 1845.

By 1820 one branch of the Scottish Lemass family had moved to Armagh and established a successful clothing business there, before moving to Dublin where they were to emulate the business success of their Huguenot ancestors. Seán Lemass amused his children by telling them they were descended from French pirates.

By 1867 John Lemass, grandfather of the future Taoiseach, had settled with his family at 2 Capel Street where he carried on trade as a hatter.

It was the year in which the Fenian rising was attempted and abandoned much as the Young Ireland rising of 1848 had been.

1

John Lemass's sympathies lay with the achievement of Irish independence through constitutional means.

He hitched his political allegiance to the rising star of County Wicklow landlord Charles Stewart Parnell and that move saw him secure a seat on Dublin Corporation. He was a member of the Irish National League, the organisation which replaced the Land League following its suppression by the British government. In April 1883 he attended a meeting of the Arran Quay Ward branch of the League at Nulty's Hotel in Dublin and seconded the resolution which proposed that a financial tribute be paid to Parnell whose County Wicklow estate was in considerable financial difficulties.

In the spring of 1885 a royal visit to Ireland by the future King Edward VII was proposed as a means of promoting loyalty to the Crown in Ireland. At a meeting of the North City Ward of Dublin burgesses John Lemass put forward the view that the citizens of the capital should maintain a dignified neutrality on the matter. As a Parnellite and nationalist it was his opinion that the city fathers should not grovel before British royalty. He sat on a committee which was set up to organise a National League demonstration against the proposed visit. When members of Dublin Corporation proposed that no loyal address be presented to the Prince of Wales on his visit, John Lemass voted for the motion. He placed his nationalist cards quite openly on the table, a move that many of his fellow Dublin businessmen of the day resolutely refused to do at a time when patronage from Dublin Castle could make or break a city businessman.

By the time his son John Timothy Lemass was born in the Capel Street premises, John Lemass senior had firmly established a flourishing business as 'purveyor of hats to the discerning'.

John Timothy inherited and expanded the family business. His hats won exhibition medals in London and in Paris and over the next half-century he established J.T. Lemass and Co as one of Dublin's leading hatters and drapers. In 1896 he married Frances Phelan, a middle-class girl from Tulore in County Offaly. A tall, attractive woman, she was four years younger than her husband.

Her family had moved to Dublin where her father, who was a horticulturist, took up a post at the Botanic Gardens in Glasnevin, while the family kept a flower shop in Wicklow Street.

During the early years of their married life the Lemasses lived over the Capel Street shop and their first child, Noel, was born there in 1897. Capel Street was the very hub of centre city commercial life – a street where attorneys-at-law practised side by side with coach-makers, chandlers and butchers. The Lemass's commercial neighbours were the stationers, Chambers and the confectioner Miss Eleanor Moran. The success of the Capel Street business brought with it a certain prosperity which allowed Frances Lemass to find a more suitable address at which to bring up her young family. They had seven children, three girls and four boys. Frances Lemass moved with her husband and first child to a quiet seaside retreat away from the bustle of inner-city life. Her second child, John Francis, was born at Norwood Cottage, Ballybrack, on 15 July 1899. He was delivered by Sarah Murphy, a midwife from Holles Street Maternity Hospital. Within 16 years of his birth the boy began to play a part in the making of modern Ireland, not as John but as Seán Lemass. But before all that there was the matter of his education.

His first school was run by the Sisters of the Holy Faith in Haddington Road some 15 minutes walk from the family home at Capel Street where they had again settled after the temporary move to Ballybrack. It was common in those days for very young boys to be educated by nuns whose principal business was the education of young Catholic ladies.

After three and a half years at Haddington Road the young Lemass returned to the north side of Dublin to continue his education. His parents chose to send him to O'Connell Schools at North Richmond Street which though run by the Christian Brothers, who educated the city's poor, was more akin to an English grammar school. The school catered predominantly for the sons of the professional middle class who decided, and perhaps could not afford, to send their children to the more élite Jesuit-run Belvedere or Clongowes Wood. The Lemasses later sent Seán's younger brother Frank to Belvedere. He married Mary MacDonagh, a niece of executed 1916 leader, Thomas MacDonagh.

At O'Connell Schools Lemass was popular because of his sporting prowess which he managed to combine with solid academic achievement. The school records show that J.F. Lemass, as he was then styled, won a first-class distinction in the examinations for the Junior Intermediate Certificate. School photographs show a handsome, sallow-skinned youth, slightly-built and of middle height. What particularly sets him apart in those photographs is the quality of his clothing. The family joked that his extremely well-cut suits were perhaps the most visible evidence that he was, after all, a draper's son.

When the young Lemass was busy grappling with the syllabus requirements for his certificate examinations others about him were not so industrious. Amongst his schoolfellows in Richmond Street was Brendan Bracken, the son of a County Tipperary stonemason, who later in life became Winston Churchill's indispensable henchman and Minister of Information in the wartime cabinet. He was, at one time, mistakenly rumoured to be the illegitimate son of Churchill – a rumour Bracken did little to quell. Bracken with his chameleon-like social skills would become as far distant from his schoolfellow as it was possible to become and they would stand firmly on opposite sides of a political chasm that only an alchemist might bridge. The future would see these Christian Brothers boys divided on a whole range of issues that would shape the future history of Ireland and of Britain.

In 1915 however, Bracken posed an altogether different threat to the young Lemass. So unruly was Bracken's behaviour in school that one teacher, a Brother Galvin, is said to have remarked that it was likely to blight Lemass's prospects of success in the Junior Intermediate examination. Such fears were misplaced because Bracken's mother soon removed him to Mungret College in Limerick and Lemass gained his first class distinction uninterrupted by the future Lord Bracken. School records show that as an Exhibitioner he took a £15 prize for

Mathematics. His other Honour subjects were English, History, Geography and he took Passes in Latin and Irish.

It was a far more significant disruption than the unruly behaviour of the precocious Brendan Bracken which was soon to clutch Lemass away from the comfortable world of his schoolfellows into the uncertain and dangerous world of revolution.

Shortly before the Easter Rising of 1916, together with his brother Noel, he joined 'A' Company, Third Battalion of the Irish Volunteers. Some of the men who worked for his father in Capel Street were already active members of the body founded in 1913. John T. Lemass supported such men and as a committed nationalist he gave a great deal of advertising to Arthur Griffith's publication *Nationality*.

The young Lemass enjoyed playing in the workshops on his father's premises listening to the talk of the skilled workmen who made the fashionable silk top hats and bowlers of that time. He recalled seeing the wooden blocks on which the individual hats were made being used to light the fire, during the fuel shortages of the First World War. Each block had the name of the owner of the hat inscribed on it, and the young boy was fascinated to see so many famous Dublin heads reach so curious an end.

In 1969 Lemass recalled how, at the age of 15½ he was recruited into the Volunteers by one of his father's employees, a man named Patrick Mullen: 'I told him I didn't think I was old enough to join and he said, "You look a great deal older than you are and this will be a white lie anyway".'

Already imbued with the nationalist fervour he had inherited from his Parnellite grandfather and father, Lemass needed very little convincing. By one of those curious coincidences the commandant of the Third Battalion was a man with whom Lemass's fortunes would be inextricably intertwined for the greater part of his life – Eamon de Valera. De Valera had risen through the ranks of the Volunteers having attended the inaugural meeting in the Rotunda in Dublin on 25 November 1913. Those who gathered in the Rotunda heard a manifesto read which left them in no doubt as to the purpose the Volunteer corps might serve in the future:

5

At a time when legislative proposals, universally confessed to be of vital concern for the future of Ireland, have been put forward, and are awaiting decision, a plan has been deliberately adopted by one of the great English political parties...to make a display of military force and the menace of armed violence the determining factor in the future relations between this country and Great Britain...such is the occasion, not altogether unfortunate, which has brought about the inception of the Irish Volunteer Movement.

Nearly 4,000 men and women joined up. De Valera later recruited young men to the Volunteers using the slogan: 'Wanted: eyes and ears for the South City battalions'. Amongst those who answered that call and who became deeply impressed with the man who was their commandant was the close on 16 year-old Seán Lemass. In later years he recalled for Michael Mills of the Irish Press his first impression of the man he would one day succeed as Taoiseach when the officer addressed 'A' Company in a basement in 41 York Street:

He had, of course, enormous personal magnetism and the capacity to hold that crowd of volunteers there while he addressed them at inordinate length as he always did. There was not a movement among the crowd until he had finished. It impressed me enormously, notwithstanding what I thought was his rather queer-looking appearance.

The somewhat confused preparations for the planned Rising were in hand from March 1915 when the Volunteer commandants met to discuss the matter. Much of the confusion which attended those preparations was born of a complicated command structure which saw the highly secretive Irish Republican Brotherhood guiding the hand of much of the Volunteer leadership. The military council of the IRB fixed the date of Easter Sunday, 23 April, for a rising to take place, but the majority of the rank and file of the Volunteers had little notion of what was afoot.

Just how much of a surprise the event was, even to its central players, is caught in a number of contemporary accounts, amongst them *The Insurrection in Dublin* by the writer James Stephens who was working in the National Gallery the day the Rising broke out: 'This has taken everyone by surprise. It is possible, that, with the exception of their staff, it has taken the Volunteers themselves by surprise...'.

Ernie O'Malley in his autobiography, *On Another Man's Wound*, captures the mood of that Easter Monday in Dublin:

> Easter Monday, a holiday, was warm and many people went to the races, to the Hill of Howth, Killiney, or to the mountains. I walked across the city...around by Dublin Castle walls. I looked at the statue of Justice on the upper Castle Gate. She had her back to the city and I remembered that it had frequently been commented on, satirically....From the flagstaff on top of the General Post Office, the GPO, floated a new flag, a tri-coloured one of green, white and orange, the colours running out from the mast. 'What's it all about?' I asked a man who stood near me, a scowl on his face. 'Those boyos, the Volunteers, have seized the Post Office. They want nothing less than a Republic,' he laughed scornfully.

In the early afternoon of Easter Monday one of those Volunteers, Gearoid O'Sullivan, had raised the tricolour which Ernie O'Malley had seen floating over the royal arms emblazoned on the pediment of the GPO. Soon afterwards, Patrick Pearse formally proclaimed the Irish Republic as the bemused citizens of the capital went about their bank holiday business.

Like so many other Volunteers confused by the cancellation orders issued by the leadership, both Seán and Noel Lemass had made other plans for the Easter Monday bank holiday. They had decided on a day trip to County Wicklow with two friends Kenneth and Jimmy O'Dea (later the distinguished comedian and lifelong friend and best man at Seán Lemass's wedding).

News of the Rising reached them on their way back from Glencree to Dublin when they met, quite by chance, the President and Commander-in-Chief of the Volunteers Eoin MacNeill. It was only by chance that, on Holy Thursday, MacNeill himself had heard of the date planned for the Rising. He was vehemently opposed to Pearse's plan, which he saw as ill-conceived at that point, and said initially that he would do all in his power, save contacting Dublin Castle, to ensure that the Rising did not go ahead as planned. He sent orders to Cork, Belfast and Limerick and sent notices to the national press cancelling the Easter Sunday mobilisation.

As they approached Rathfarnham, on Easter Monday, the Lemass brothers spoke to MacNeill, who dampened somewhat their youthful zeal for revolution. Lemass described MacNeill's condition:

> Professor MacNeill seemed agitated and depressed. He informed us that the Volunteers had occupied various positions in the city, but he had no information as to further events. He was very clearly unhappy about the whole situation.

The nearest position was at Jacob's biscuit factory commanding the southern approach to the city centre but on that Monday they were unable to locate their own battalion which was then in Ringsend. To de Valera, who was seriously short of manpower in Boland's Mills, even those inexperienced boys would no doubt have been a welcome sight.

Undaunted, they scouted the city on Tuesday, stopping first at the Four Courts on the quays near their father's shop. There they learned the whereabouts of de Valera and his men but they were prevented from joining up with the fellows of their battalion. When the Lemass brothers reached the spot at the GPO where, less than 24 hours earlier Patrick Pearse had declared a Republic, they were ushered inside.

They informed the first officer they met of their reason for missing the mobilisation and of how they were unable to meet up with their own battalion. At this point the brothers were separated. Noel was sent to the Imperial Hotel on the other side of the street where he served under Gerald Crofts and suffered gunshot wounds later in the week. Seán was absorbed into the GPO garrison, armed with a shotgun and some home-made bombs and sent to the roof of the GPO. He was positioned at a corner nearest Nelson's Pillar and was under the command of a Volunteer officer called Cremin who had come from London to take part in the Rising.

Throughout his life Seán Lemass rarely referred to his personal involvement in the events of that week. Charles Haughey recalled that the only time he heard Lemass speak of this period was when travelling by car with him through the countryside. If they passed a site associated with those days he might just make a 'passing reference to it'. From one brief published account of his own, and from contemporary accounts, many of which are clouded over by a green haze, we learn that he stood at his post as bidden, when required to fire he handled his gun with a calm resolute air, and though noticeably shy, the boy soldier won the affection of his older comrades. His own view of his days in the GPO was simply that he did not consider himself a hero nor did he wished to be considered by others as one.

On the Saturday of Easter Week, Pearse and his men had been forced to evacuate the burning GPO and an attempt was made to enter into negotiations with the British for an unconditional surrender. That attempt failed. Lemass and a group of other Volunteers left the GPO for a warehouse yard near Moore Street. Before he left he performed one task of which he later wrote:

> Many people have claimed to have helped in carrying the wounded Connolly from the GPO. In fact, the process was so slow and so frequently interrupted, that almost everyone in the GPO helped in it at some stage. Personally, I assisted to carry Connolly's stretcher for a short distance to a small door opening on Henry Street, where however I was ordered, with all those around, to proceed at the run up the small back street, Moore Lane, opposite the GPO.

He remembered those moments after the surrender when he and his colleagues made their way through burned-out and looted shops:

> While waiting in the yard, I experienced both hunger and fatigue. I ate a tin of preserved fruit from a shop through which we had passed, and while seated on the stairway into the yard, watching the obstacles being removed, I fell asleep for a few moments.

He woke some minutes later to hear Seán McDermott address the men on the decision to surrender and recalled later: 'He spoke briefly but very movingly and many of those present were weeping.' Lemass and the other survivors then paraded in single column out of the yard and into Moore Street under the Volunteer flag and the white flag of surrender. He spent a cold night in the overcrowded grounds of the Rotunda Hospital before being transferred the next day to Richmond Barracks at the city's western extremity. De Valera was there too, awaiting his sentence of deportation.

Various accounts exist of how Lemass was released from captivity. Up to the 12 May, 206 men were released. According to his own account, he spent about a fortnight in custody after the Rising before being sent home with a group of youngsters who were in or around his own age. The family recall that his mother went to plead for his release. Yet another account has it that a member of the Dublin Metropolitan Police, who knew the family, intervened to save him from deportation. When the DMP man identified Lemass a British officer is said to have looked at his watch and told the boy: 'You have ten minutes to get out of here.' Lemass's own account, though less romantic, is the more likely. According to *The Irish Times Handbook of the Rising*, Lemass's case was 'fully investigated'. Public opinion in Ireland had taken a remarkable turn in favour of the insurgents after the execution of the leaders of the Rising. There was little to be gained from detaining a handful of 16 year-old boys longer than was necessary.

Two weeks after the chance encounter which led him to the GPO, the boy soldier, Seán Lemass, returned home. His relieved parents welcomed them and chastised the recklessness of their two sons. Apart from fatigue Seán was unscathed but Noel had been wounded in the hand in the fighting at the Imperial Hotel. His father was proud that they had taken the stand they did but with a sensible eye to the future he had other things in mind for Seán at this time. Just over two months after his son's release from Richmond Barracks Lemass senior insisted that he return to Rosse College – where he had already been briefly in attendance before the Rising – so that he might study for his matriculation examination. This was with a view to his reading for the Bar. When he complained he was reminded by his father that he would not be the first revolutionary to be a barrister. Patrick Pearse had been a member of the profession. His father also insisted that he work in the family business and for some years to come this was Lemass's only source of income. In the 1940s he confided to a friend that he barely managed to contain his anger at his parents decision to force him back to school against his own wishes. His father and mother were concerned but tolerant of his involvement in the Volunteers. His daughters recall that Lemass cousins of their grandfather's disapproved so much of Seán and Noel's activities that they cut all contact with the family. They remember that the feud continued when they were children and they had no contact with that side of the family until many years later.

By January 1917 Lemass had abandoned his studies again for the more active life of the Volunteers, then reorganising after the Rising. He now joined 'C' Company, Second Battalion and was rapidly promoted first lieutenant. He served under Seán Colbert who was company captain. He began to spend less and less time in his father's shop and though still on the payroll most of his energy went into training the Volunteers under his command.

At the end of 1917 de Valera was made president of the Volunteers and the process of unification of the political and military factions of the organisation got underway. Also in 1917 the somewhat disparate elements which constituted Sinn Féin were united into a more effective pan-nationalist political machine which successfully fought a series of by-elections across the country. So successful was the process that by the end of 1917 Sinn Féin had established over 1,200 branches. By this time the Irish Party – reeling from the blows dealt it by the Home Rule debate and the conscription crisis – had lost the initiative. By April 1918 the threat of conscription hung firmly over the country and a revamped Sinn Féin seized the moment to political advantage.

The reorganised party's first major test was the general election of December 1918. Sinn Féin won a landslide victory but refused to take their seats at Westminster. Instead in January 1919 it constituted itself as Dáil Éireann with de Valera at its head and Arthur Griffith as his deputy. On 21 January 1919 a Declaration of Irish Independence was issued in Irish, English and French, to the governments of the world. On democratic principles the representative nature of the assembly could not be denied. The assertion of national self-consciousness through the Sinn Féin victory and their subsequent Declaration of a Republic was received in London with studied indifference. Such indifference was reflected in the lack of editorial comment in the British press.

The Irish Times gave comfort to its Unionist readers when it wrote of the First Dáil's Declaration as 'a solemn act of defiance of the British Empire by a body of young men who have not the slightest notion of that Empire's power and resources. The more quickly Ireland becomes convinced of the folly which elected them, the sooner sanity will return.'

While this new political force forged ahead with what London saw as theatrical gestures, Lemass continued to be immersed in Volunteer activities.

When the Dublin Brigade Convention of the Volunteers was held in 1919 he was one of two delegates sent to represent his company. He was charged with the task of raising the controversial matter of the carrying of arms during Volunteer parades, a matter his own company felt particularly strong about. The men resented the fact that they were allowed carry nothing more lethal than stout sticks, which they felt, made them look more like cattle drovers than soldiers. The resolution was not debated at the Convention and when Lemass brought that news to a meeting of 'C' Company they threatened to resign *en masse*.

At a private meeting with General Liam Lynch at 44 North Great Georges Street, Dublin, Lemass was later informed that the matter would be referred to Volunteer GHQ. Two weeks later permission to carry arms was granted to Lemass's company and quite soon after it became common practice at Volunteer parades.

In August 1919 the Dáil approved a motion which called on the Volunteers to formally swear allegiance to the Republic and to the Dáil. It was felt, especially by Arthur Griffith and Cathal Brugha, that such a move would establish the authority of the Dáil over the movement and would also help break the IRB's stranglehold on elements of the Volunteers. In 1920 the Volunteers became officially known as the Irish Republican Army.

In October 1920 Liberal Prime Minister Lloyd George promised to break up 'the small body of assassins, a real murder gang, dominating the country and terrorising it'. When he spoke those words the ministers of the Dáil had already gone underground and guerilla warfare was raging haphazardly in Ireland. The first shots of 'the troubles' – the euphemism for the Anglo-Irish War and its aftermath – were fired in Soloheadbeg, County Tipperary, where two policemen were killed. Much of the fighting was concentrated in the Munster area. The war which began early in 1919 and ran to July 1921 further embittered the already troubled course of Anglo-Irish relations. While it occasioned savage brutality on both sides, there were no large-scale engagements and the loss of life in relative terms was small.

When 'the troubles' began the main activity of Lemass's company was confined to raids for arms. He also commanded a somewhat unusual raid in Dublin to recover £500 worth of stolen jewellery snatched by a gang of thieves whose best interests were not those of the Republic.

He continued the intensive training of his men in the Dublin mountains and by the end of 1920 he was acting captain in his company following the illness of Seán Colbert. He began to show signs of the administrative skills he would later use as a minister and was chosen to organise a major part of the 'boycott Belfast goods' campaign which was launched as a reprisal for attacks on Catholics in that city.

When he took time out from his revolutionary activities it was to pursue one of his principal leisure interests – amateur drama. He was a member of a group called the Kilronan Players and on Sunday 11 January 1920 he played the part of Sir Lucius O'Trigger in their production of Richard Brinsley Sheridan's five act comedy *The Rivals*. Under the auspices of the Irish Dramatic Union the play was produced at the Abbey Theatre and the cast included his future best man, Jimmy O'Dea.

At this time he was also seeing his future wife Kathleen Hughes who had been his childhood sweetheart. Their families were friendly through shared vacations at the seaside at Skerries where they took summer villas. However, the Hughes parents considered Lemass an unsuitable boyfriend for their daughter. The family was not as steeped in nationalist politics as the Lemass family had been since the nineteenth century. In fact they were more concerned that their daughter should make a suitable match than that Ireland should become a republic. Agnes and Thomas Hughes did not consider the 'cap-wearing revolutionary', as they called Lemass, to be a suitable candidate for their daughter's hand. Thomas Hughes was a conservative, middle-class Roman Catholic who worked as a carpet buyer at Arnotts department store. He and his wife lived all of their married life in Beechwood Avenue, in the comfortable suburb of Ranelagh. They were dismayed to see their daughter collected by an IRA man in the side-car of his motorbike. Their protestations went unheard, Kathleen was determined to marry Seán Lemass.

While staying with his family in early December 1920, Lemass was arrested and interned with other republicans in Ballykinlar, County Down, where he spent the next year.

Concerned for his safety and unsure of his whereabouts, his father wrote to Dublin Castle on 7 December. He received this curt and formal reply from a Major Fitzpatrick on 10 December:

> Re. John Lemass
> I regret to say that your son is on Michael Collin's *(sic)* List
> and is graded as a Lieutenant in the IRA.

For the greater part of the year his home was camp number 1, hut 26. Amongst his fellow inmates in hut 26, were two Dungannon brothers, Charles and Dan Cavanagh. Charles Cavanagh remembered Lemass as 'a small quiet Dublin fellow who spent most of his time reading books on economics'. Cavanagh kept an autograph book from those days in which Lemass inscribed the following verse by Denis Florence McCarthy:

> As long as Ireland hears the chink of bare ignoble chains
> As long as one detested link of foreign rule remains
> As long as our rightful debt one smallest fraction's due
> So long, my friends, there's something yet
> For Irishmen to do.

At Ballykinlar the inmates set up such a range of classes that their nickname for the institution was 'the university'. They also circulated a newspaper and even issued their own coinage. One of the inmates in Ballykinlar, Hugh Early, many years later, became the driver of Lemass's state car.

Liam Skinner in a somewhat romantic view of Lemass in his book *Politicians By Accident* quotes this view of him held by another internee:

> ...a very quiet, unassuming young fellow, showing an insatiable appetite for books on history and economics. Games held, very little, if any appeal for him. He was too busy making up for the education lost by his entry into the movement.

Lemass was released from Ballykinlar in December 1921. Release from the camp did not always mean a safe passage home. On 16 November 1921 Alderman Tadgh Barry from Cork was shot dead by a trigger-happy, eighteen year old sentry, as he prepared to leave with a group of released internees. Lemass ordered the Cavanagh brothers to take the body in from the place where it fell.

The trains carrying released internees from Ballykinlar were sometimes stoned by Unionist mobs at Portadown. Some of the internees who worked for organisations like the Great Northern Railway were refused their old jobs on release.

Skinner gives us this description of Lemass after his release from Ballykinlar: 'At this time he invariably wore a cap, riding breeches and leggings, was clean shaven and smoked a pipe. He often invited his comrades to Capel Street for debates.'

There, in a back room in his father's shop, a hardcore of IRA activists debated the question which was to see the country and the young Lemass caught in the jaws of a bitter civil war.

A truce with the British had been arranged in July 1921 while Lemass was still interned. On 6 December, after intense negotiations, a treaty was signed by the Dáil's plenipotentiaries and British ministers. The 26 counties were granted dominion status. The terms of the agreement did not apply to the six counties of Northern Ireland. The Irish representatives brought back from London, not the republic that had been sought by so many, but 'freedom to achieve freedom'. It was a freedom which Seán O'Faoláin characterised as 'the dream that went bust'.

The cleavage in republican ranks caused by the signing of the Treaty deeply affected Lemass but he did not rush immediately to support one side or the other. It was not until the Dáil ratified the Treaty by a slim majority that he made up his mind on where he stood. He found the oath of allegiance to the British Crown unacceptable and above all he objected to the other restrictions the agreement placed on the achievement of absoulte independence. He decided very firmly in support of the anti-Treaty side. For a very brief period he had served as a training officer to the newly formed Gárda Síochána, a position he soon abandoned as incompatible with his stance on the Treaty.

If the GPO was the symbol most closely associated with the Rising, it was the Four Courts that was the symbolic heartland of the anti-Treaty forces during the Civil War. The building was only a few hundred yards from the Lemass shop in Capel Street. It had been a port of call for Lemass when he was seeking out his Volunteer companions in 1916. When Gandon's architectural masterpiece was occupied by anti-Treaty forces in the spring of 1922 Lemass moved in with the majority of his company and was appointed Barrack Adjutant. He joined Liam Mellows, Paddy O'Brien, Bob Briscoe, Todd Andrews and other officers of the occupying garrison. Andrews remembered him as a strict disciplinarian with a reserved manner which helped him keep firm control of the men under his command.

The eleven-month Civil War claimed over six times as many nationalist lives as had been killed by British forces in the five year period between the Easter Rising and the signing of the Treaty.

When the Four Courts fell on 30 June 1922 Lemass led his men out past the crowds gathered outside, amongst them his brother Frank. He was taken to a disused distillery which belonged to Jameson's in Stoneybatter. There the same good fortune which attended him in 1916 did not desert him now. Liam Skinner describes how Lemass made good his escape from the distillery yard:

> On the opposite side of the yard, into which the prisoners were led, there was a door. After some time, it was discovered that it had been left unlocked. Seán Lemass, Ernie O'Malley, Joe Griffin, Paddy Rigney and a fifth prisoner walked through the door, made their way into the street, and mixed with the populace.

Lemass later described this time as one which lacked direction and firm leadership. He lost no time in rejoining active service. He first attempted to join the Wicklow Brigade, failed to make contact but later joined up with republicans from Tipperary who were in Blessington, County Wicklow. He was appointed to headquarters staff of the Eastern Command and served in Wexford and Carlow. In July 1922 Lemass was with a group of over 200 Irregulars who attacked the Free State stronghold of Enniscorthy, County Wexford. The plan was to starve out the garrisons in the castle and the barracks in order to avoid unnecessary loss of life. Lemass lost one of his close comrades, Commandant Paddy O'Brien, within the shadow of Enniscorthy Barracks which they had set out to reconnoitre.

In the autumn of 1922 Lemass was given the job of establishing an intelligence network for the republicans but he had hardly set about the task when, in December, he was arrested, and again the place of his arrest was just a few hundred yards from his family's business premises on the quays near O'Connell Bridge. He was interned at two locations. First he was taken to Harepark Camp, the Curragh and after trying to escape from there, to Mountjoy.

As at Ballykinlar, he set about the process of self-education in economics, which was to continue for many years to come. He became quite introverted and did not mix much with the other internees at Mountjoy. A brusqueness of manner became more pronounced during his time in Mountjoy. Some inmates saw it as a protective shield to cover a natural shyness; others saw it as a natural tendency to be assertive and insensitive to the opinion of others, especially during debate on political matters.

By early 1923 the anti-Treaty cause had been effectively defeated. The military defeat was devastating for the republicans but its effect on their morale paled into insignificance beside the blow dealt them by the electorate. In 1922 and in 1923 the electorate voted to accept the Treaty. The result of the 1922 election gave rise to de Valera's haunting phrase when he said 'the majority had no right to do wrong'. Other republicans saw the result as the product of British coercion because, they claimed, the British threatened war if the Treaty was not accepted. In the 1923 election the result was the same.

Dr Tom Garvin sees that result as a serious body blow to the IRA, especially to those members who saw that the republic of their dreams was dead and who might now be contemplating another direction:

In 1923, after the Civil War, the electorate voted preponderantly for pro-Treaty parties and the message was unambiguous. The entire IRA campaign of 1919-21 had been legitimised in the minds of the Dáil and IRA leaderships as being in accordance with the will of the electorate as expressed in December 1918. It was difficult to ignore that electorate when it turned on them....Eventually the less militarised or educable of the anti-Treatyites absorbed the bitter lesson of 1922-23; military defeat, electoral unpopularity and four years in the political wilderness were good teachers...

Lemass was already learning these lessons in Mountjoy. The news coming from outside to the prisoner in Mountjoy did much to shape the direction of his political re-education. However, at this time he was still a diehard republican with little time for what he saw as the posturing of politicians.

In October 1923 circumstances conspired yet again to free Lemass from internment. This time however the circumstances were a matter of family tragedy. He was released on parole to attend the funeral of his brother Noel who had been arrested on 3 July and brutally murdered.

Six days after the arrest his father wrote to the Lord Mayor of Dublin:

Could you find out for me the whereabouts of my son Noel D. Lemass? He returned to Ireland a few days ago after an absence of eight months and was arrested in Exchequer St on Tuesday July 3. He was in the company of Mr Divine of the Corporation at the time. As I have not heard from him I am anxious about him.

Though separated through their IRA activities the Lemass brothers remained in close contact through the organisation's communications network and whenever possible they would arrange meetings at the family home. Noel was more social than his younger brother and played a more active role in both the Rising and the War of Independence. He trained as an engineer and when arrested for his part in the War of Independence in 1920 he was employed at the Municipal Workshops in Dublin. He was handsome and popular and more outgoing than his brother. He took a fatherly interest in his young sisters. Peggy Lemass remembers her aunt Claire telling her that when she had an unsuitable boyfriend Noel was usually the one who sent him packing. One such suitor gave Claire a gold watch which Noel insisted that she return. When she did so he replaced the watch for her at his own expense. Noel was engaged for a brief period to Lena Roddy, who later married the Mayo solicitor P.J. Ruttledge, who served in cabinet with Seán Lemass.

Before he met his death in the shadow of the Hell Fire Club in the Dublin Mountains, Noel Lemass was no stranger to internment camps and prisons. As a prisoner in Mountjoy he wrote to his boss at the Corporation Works, P.J. Monks, on November 27, 1919:

> Dear Mr Monks,
> I have been sentenced to twelve months imprisonment with hard labour for illegal drilling etc. and as a result shall be unable to be at work for some time. I would be very much obliged if you would arrange with the committee that I would receive leave of absence for a period not longer than one year. The Lord Mayor calls here to see the prisoners and has been very kind to me. We look upon him as a kind of fairy godmother.

He was transferred to prison in Derry on the 7 February 1920 and his sentence expired on the 14 November. An order for his arrest was issued again on 2 June 1921. It stated that he was a person 'suspected of acting, having acted, and being about to act in a manner prejudicial to the restoration and maintenance of order in Ireland'.

Noel Lemass's body was discovered in October 1923 in the Dublin Mountains. He was considered a prize target by certain elements within the CID who were fanatical supporters of Michael Collins. They operated out of the Criminal Investigation Department at Oriel House and would have certainly known that

Seán Lemass had planned an attack on their HQ just before he was arrested near O'Connell Bridge and sent to the Curragh.

Noel Lemass was suspected by Michael Collins of interfering with his mail but more important was the fact that he was the chief suspect in the murder of Seán Hales, a TD and close friend of Collins, shot in reprisal for the execution of Erskine Childers and other republicans. No proof has ever emerged of Noel Lemass's involvement in the shooting of Hales but in those troubled times the finger of suspicion was more than enough for his enemies to kill someone they saw as a hardcore and ruthless IRA man.

The killing of his brother had a profound effect on Seán Lemass.

Acting on information, the Guards began a dragging operation on sections of the River Liffey beginning at Ballyward Bridge near Blessington on 10 October. Three days later the newspapers reported the discovery of the body. It was found, not in the Liffey, but on a bleak patch of mountainside near the Hell Fire Club. It was decomposed and there were two bullet wounds to the skull. Parts of the fingers, some teeth and hair were found some distance from the body. John T. and Frances Lemass went to the scene and were only able to identify it as their son's from the remains of his clothes. Mrs Lemass told the *Saturday Herald,* 'It is a terrible end after all he did for his country'. She also told the paper that when the split came after the Treaty was signed, her son 'refused to fight his own'.

An unusual and somewhat inconclusive inquest on Noel's death opened in Rathmines Town Hall on 15 October 1923.

According to the Coroner, Dr J.P. Brennan, the business of the inquest would be to find out, if possible, who killed Noel Lemass. It failed in its terms of reference. Within days of the opening submissions the inquest was making banner headlines in the national press. A crowded public gallery saw J.A. Costello, barrister, represent the State and amongst the witnesses called was General Eoin O'Duffy founder of the Blueshirts. Sensational evidence was given in the course of the inquest. It was alleged that witnesses were issued with death threats variously by Free State army officers, members of the Central Intelligence Division of the Civic Guards and IRA officers. The claims were never substantiated and the inquest failed to identify the killer of Noel Lemass.

Seán Lemass's daughter Sheila recalls that at some point during his career her father discovered the identity of his brother's killer and worked with the man, but revealed his identity only to his wife Kathleen. One of the names mentioned in connection with the murder of Noel Lemass was that of Emmet Dalton, who founded Ardmore Film Studios. Dalton was with Michael Collins when he was shot and the finger of suspicion has been pointed at him even in relation to that killing. No solid evidence has emmerged to support the claim that he had anything to do with the murder of Noel Lemass. One thing however, may have connected him with the murder. Soon after the death of Collins, Hazel, Lady Lavery, wife of the painter Sir John Lavery, wrote to Dalton informing him that Collins told her that he suspected Noel Lemass of interfering with his mail. As a result, Collins said he felt his movements were being successfuly monitored by his enemies. Hazel Lavery was passionately in love with Collins or at least infatuated by him. A casual comment from Lady Lavery, whom it seems was as witless as she was beautiful, may have cost Noel Lemass his life.

There is yet another reason why Noel Lemass may have met such an early and tragic death, but again at this remove we can only speculate. It is possible that Noel Lemass may have been targeted by the CID because of his brother's plans to blow up their HQ. Seán Lemass's plans to attack Oriel House were discovered, the plot foiled and he was arrested. From evidence presented at the Noel Lemass inquest it appears that many instructions issued by the fledgling CID were vague in the extreme. Seán's role in the Civil War was very much more active than Noel's and as a target would have been more highly prized than his older brother. If he became aware of the fact that his own plans for CID HQ played a role in his brother's death, the burden of such knowledge would have been intolerable for a man of Seán Lemass's devotion to family. Charles Haughey recalls that when he became Minister for

Justice in 1961 Lemass told him to find out all he could about the murder of Kevin O'Higgins but he did not make a similar request about his brother's killers. The pain of that memory ran deep. What is certain is, his brother's murder left an indelible scar on Seán Lemass. It was one of the decisive factors which steered him away from the mores of a gunman to the politics of the ballot box. For the rest of his life Lemass kept in his possession a drawing done by his brother in Mountjoy Jail. It depicts three Volunteers rushing from a darkened room with bayonets fixed. It represented a world which Seán Lemass had decided to leave behind.

2

POLITICAL APPRENTICESHIP

Lemass's absorption into the political wing of the republican movement occurred without his knowledge or consent on the day of his brother's funeral. The Sinn Féin Árd Fheis of 1923 was in session on the October day when Noel Lemass was buried. The chairman called for the session to be suspended so that delegates could attend the funeral. The following day Lemass read in the newspapers that he had been elected to the organisation's Standing Committee – the body which was the senior administrative arm of the party. His first reaction was one of utter indignation that he should be elected to such a body without consultation and as a sentimental reaction to the tragedy of his brother's death.

His indignation soon turned to a more practical outlook and he began to immerse himself in the functions of membership of the Standing Committee. He attended his first meeting on 4 December 1923 and thereafter he was a regular attender until the eve of the foundation of Fianna Fáil when the members of the new party withdrew.

In the spring of the following year he began to show the first signs of the awakening of a political intelligence. It took the form of committing his thoughts on political organisation to print in the party's oracle *An Phoblacht*. His political journalism began rather humbly with a request to the editor to publish some photographs. On 7 April 1924 he wrote from Sinn Féin HQ, 23 Suffolk Street, requesting the publication of photographs of Volunteers, the anniversary of whose deaths occurred at that time. He also informed the editor that he was compiling a souvenir book containing the photos of all men killed since January 1922. Soon this mundane editorial work was replaced with more serious political journalism but first he turned his attention to his personal life.

His father had continued to support him financially throughout his periods of internment. He did this in the belief that if his son was still on the payroll at 2 Capel Street it provided at least some cover, albeit a somewhat transparent one, for the well-known IRA man. In early 1924 Lemass returned more or less full-time to the family business but his heart was most definitely not in the manufacture of top hats. He would often be found in the store rooms surrounded by rows of boxed 'toppers' wistfully drawing on a cigarette and gazing into the middle distance.

If his heart was not with the family business it was certainly with his fiancée Kathleen Hughes. He married her in August 1924 despite her parent's objections. They had seen very little of one another before they married but she had corresponded with him throughout his two periods of internment and their courtship lasted for eight years. When he was picked up by Free State troops near O'Connell Bridge she had seen him pass, under arrest, as she stood waiting to cross the road at Dame Street where she worked as a secretary with the GEC. Their social life was extremely limited. She was in the audience of the Abbey Theatre to see him play Sir Lucius O'Trigger but they hardly ever went to a dance in Dublin. That was to leave Lemass a slightly embarrassed wallflower when he later exchanged the Volunteer uniform for white tie and tails. In later years he amused the wives of various heads of state with what they must have seen as a curious excuse for being unable to dance with them at state receptions.

He married Kathleen Hughes at 6 a.m. with only the bridesmaid Gertrude O'Dea, best man Jimmy O'Dea, family, and a handful of friends present. The reason for the early start was to enable them to catch the 8 a.m. mail-boat which would set them on their way to London, their honeymoon destination. Lemass sold the motorbike with side-car, which so annoyed his father-in-law, to pay for the honeymoon. Kathleen Lemass recalled towards the end of her life that her husband was somewhat uneasy about being in London. She recalled him dragging her out of a theatre when the band struck up 'God Save the King'. The couple returned to Dublin and set up home at Rookby Road, Terenure. Their first child Maureen was born on 25 September 1925. She was followed by Peggy in May 1927, Sheila in October 1932 and Noel in February 1928.

Over the two years following his marriage, Lemass wrote an incisive series of articles for *An Phoblacht* which indicated his changing political philosophy and prophesised the declining fortunes of what historians call the Third Sinn Féin.

A majority of republicans at this time held the view that the Second Dáil had never been dissolved. The vexed question of abstention from the Free State legislature had dogged the republican ranks. For many abstention was a matter of principle on which they refused to budge. De Valera, however, after his release from Arbour Hill Prison on 16 July 1924 was prepared to concede that the recognition of the Free State parliament by the majority of the people gave it a *de facto* title. Lemass shared this view. The oath of allegiance to the British monarch which deputies were required to sign before taking their seats in the Dáil generated a more emotional debate. The oath read:

I...do solemnly swear true faith and allegiance to the Constitution of the Irish Free State as by law established and that I will be faithful to H.M. King George V, his heirs and successors by law, in virtue of the common citizenship of Ireland with Great Britain and her adherence to and membership of the group of nations forming the British Commonwealth of Nations.

The Cosgrave government's insistence that the oath be administered, was part of its policy of adhering to the strict letter of the Treaty signed with Britain. It was one of the more minor provisions of the Treaty which, for Cosgrave's government, in the wake of the Civil War, took on a significance disproportionate to what it should have represented.

Two issues dominated Sinn Féin's agenda. Lemass would soon be concerned with the practicalities of both. He would be supporting de Valera's views on the question of the role of the Second Dáil and the oath of allegiance. De Valera made known his views on these issues soon after his release from Arbour Hill Prison.

Within a month of his release de Valera called a meeting of those Sinn Féin deputies elected to the Second Dáil and at the subsequent general election. He asked the meeting to ratify Comhairle na d'Teachtai, the Council of Deputies, as the actual government of Ireland. The Second Dáil would remain as the *de jure* government and legislature as a matter of continuity but the Council of State would be the actual government of the country. De Valera's biographer Tim Pat Coogan sees the effect of the creation of the Comhairle as:

> ...instead of having both feet firmly off the ground in the wraiths of the Second Dáil, the Council now only had one. It was at least something which existed, even though it had nothing of political substance, and it looked to de Valera, not to the Second Dáil, as the fountainhead of authority.

De Valera's prevarication on the question of signing the oath of allegiance is much travelled territory. An indication of which direction de Valera and Lemass might take on the oath in the future was given when de Valera returned to Ennis in 1925, a year after his arrest there. He told the crowd gathered to hear him: 'Things may be forced on us, we may temporarily have to submit to certain things, but our assent they can never have.'

By this time Lemass had been elected a TD. In March 1924 he was selected as Sinn Féin candidate to contest a by-election in South Dublin caused by the death of Philip Cosgrave. As with his appointment to the Standing Committee of Sinn Féin he learned of his selection as a candidate from the newspapers and again he expressed resentment, later tempered with pride, at the lack of consultation. With many republicans still in prison and a somewhat lacklustre and inefficient first campaign, Lemass fáiled to gain the seat. His performance was quite creditable given it was his first time out. His main opponent, James O'Meara of Cumann na nGaedheal, polled 17,193 and Lemass 13,492.

His second chance in the same constituency came sooner than expected. The appointment of Hugh Kennedy to the post of Chief Justice caused the by-election. After securing the Sinn Féin nomination for the November election Lemass was determined to take on the management of his own campaign. The hard edge of his republican principles was still evident from an election speech he made in front of the old parliament building in College Green when those assembled heard him say:

> ...when the Republicans come into control of the machinery of government it will be moved in the interests of the whole Irish people and not in the interests of a small privileged class.

The Irish Times reported him telling an election rally in College Street that his party believed that compromise had failed and that their object was complete independence for the whole of Ireland. That, he said, was the only way stability would be secured.

Lemass canvased support from all kinds of groups including the Council for the Unemployed who endorsed his candidacy. His strategy worked. He polled nearly 1,000 votes more than his Cumann na nGaedheal rival Séamus Hughes. The final result was Lemass 17,297; Hughes 16,340. His success in mobilising the republican vote was acknowledged by *The Irish Times* which put his success down to a low turn-out of government supporters. After his election he told the voters of South City: 'As long as you stand by the Republic, I will represent you.'

He was 25 years old. Lemass remained a public representative for the next 41 years.

Five by-elections, including the one in which Lemass won his first seat, were held on 18 November. Sinn Féin won two of the five seats gaining nearly 30,000 votes more that it did in the same constituencies in 1923. In Lemass's constituency he doubled the Sinn Féin vote and was catapulted into national prominence at a rate which seemed to surprise the candidate himself more than anyone else.

By March 1925 Sinn Féin had 48 unoccupied seats in Leinster House. At this time party support was beginning to drift towards those with real political power and who were in effect the decision makers. Elected representatives who made a virtue of holding out for the Republic through a policy of abstention, did little to reassure constituents who were beset by the problems attending the harsh economic realities of mid-1920s Ireland.

Lemass's disillusionment with Sinn Féin manifested itself openly in October 1925 in an article in *An Phoblacht*. He made a harsh attack on the incompetence of party officials and called for a major organisational shake-up of the party. He was well placed to make such a call. De Valera had appointed him to the sub-committee on organisation set up in a vain attempt to rationalise the Sinn Féin executive. As chairman of a seven-member reorganisation committee for Dublin city and county he exhorted the younger members to 'weed out the duds'. He was also drawing on his administrative experience as Frank Aiken's replacement as titular Minister for Defence in the government which republicans recognised as the legitimate government of Ireland.

Within the party ranks, debate on its policy of abstention intensified. A day before the first anniversary of Lemass's election to the Dáil, on 17 November, the Sinn Féin Árd Fheis hotly debated the party's abstention policy. Some delegates, aware that the tide was turning against abstention, proposed the following resolution:

> Owing to the insidious rumours that Republicans will enter the Free State Parliament if the Oath be removed, we call on Sinn Féin to get a definite statement from the Government that they will adhere to the policy of Cathal Brugha, Erskine Childers, and their fellow martyrs, and enter only a Republican Parliament for all Ireland.

De Valera was opposed to the terms of the motion and with the support of Lemass and Countess Markievicz he pushed through an amendment which proposed a compromise. It proposed that no change in current policy be made but 'no subject of discussion is barred' except the 'questions of accepting allegiance to a foreign king and the partition of Ireland'. It was passed by a majority vote.

Just three days before the Árd Fheis met, the IRA severed all connections with de Valera's shadow government. At an IRA convention on 14 November Peadar O'Donnell's Donegal Battalion moved this resolution:

> That in view of the fact that the Government has developed into a mere political party and has apparently lost sight of the fact that all our energies should be devoted to the all-important work of making the Army efficient so that the renegades who, through a *coup d'etat*, assumed governmental powers in this country be dealt with at the earliest possible opportunity, the Army of the Republic sever its connection with the Dáil, and act under an independent Executive, such Executive be given the power to declare war, when in its opinion, a suitable opportunity arises to rid the Republic of its enemies and maintain it in accordance with the proclamation of 1916.

Brian Farrell, in his biography of Lemass, makes this observation of his attitude to that decision:

> Lemass had little regard for this rump IRA's dream of another offensive campaign. He was increasingly conscious of the need to organise and mobilise public opinion. The break with the army mirrored growing tensions in his attitude to, and relations with, Sinn Féin.

At the 14 November convention Frank Aiken said there had been talk amongst some elements of the leadership about entering Leinster House if the issue of the oath of allegiance could be resolved. The meeting erupted in outraged disbelief at what the hardcore republicans saw as treacherous talk and Aiken and his supporters were removed from office. When O'Donnell's motion was carried the debate on abstention entered a new phase.

Comhairle na dTeachtai met on 18 December and de Valera proposed that Sinn Féin should move to have the oath of allegiance abolished so they could take up their seats in Leinster House without compromise to their republican principles.

De Valera's view, for which he had the backing of Lemass, was put to the Sinn Féin membership thus:

> That once the admission oath of the Twenty-Six–County and Six-County assemblies is removed, it becomes a question not of principle but of policy whether or not Republican representatives should attend these assemblies.

De Valera's viewpoint was not acceptable to the majority. It was an important test for his position of realising the Republic as quickly as possible but he did not prevail. Father Michael O'Flanagan proposed an amendment to de Valera's motion which read: 'That it is incompatible with the fundamental principle of Sinn Féin to send representatives into any usurping legislature set up by English law in Ireland.'

Sinn Féin was not willing to accept the new direction favoured by de Valera and Lemass. Father O'Flanagan's motion was carried but by a slim majority of 223 votes to 218. As Tim Pat Coogan has put it 'after three days of debate Sinn Féin had demonstrated clearly that it wanted the man but not his policy'. For de Valera this was not enough and he did not conceal his disappointment:

> This is the opportune time, and I realise that the coming general election is the time…I am from this moment a free man… my duty as President of this organisation is ended….

The Father O'Flanagan vote occasioned what Countess Markievicz called 'an unholy row'. She wrote to her sister Eva Gore-Booth at this time:

> Dev, I say like a wise man, has announced that he will go into the Free State Parliament if there is no oath….I myself have always said that the oath made it absolutely impossible

for an honourable person who is a republican to go in, and that if it were removed it would then be simply a question of policy with no principle involved whether we went in or stayed out....Some unlogical persons are howling. They stand for principle and for the honour of the Republic and prefer to do nothing but shout continually 'The Republic Lives'.

Lemass was at the vanguard of a core of pragmatists who were anxious to escape the bleating histrionics of fundamentalists like Father O'Flanagan. Tom Garvin in *The Evolution of Irish Nationalist Politics* remarks that O'Flanagan had been 'a visible symbol of the unity between Irish Catholicism and purist republicanism'. For Lemass the priest typified much that was wrong with Sinn Féin. He saw him as being 'under the impression that he was a kind of spiritual chaplain and political pope to the Sinn Féin Organisation, and that as long as he was alive he was under the impression that the continuity of the Organisation was represented by him'.

To lessen the sting of the rejection of de Valera's proposal Father O'Flanagan and others proposed that the Árd Fheis pay tribute to de Valera as 'the greatest Irishman for a century'. He was in no mood for such compliments. The day after the vote, de Valera, who had been President of Sinn Féin since 1917 announced his decision to resign. De Valera's resignation was the catalyst for the formation of a new political force which would replace Sinn Féin as the major republican opposition to Cumann na nGaedheal but the suggestion for its formation came not from de Valera but from Lemass. Lemass was now convinced more than ever that rump Sinn Féin would remain suspended between constitutional politics and the militant factions of the IRA. He later recalled that at this time he thought the public image of Sinn Féin was being affected by a 'galaxy of cranks' around it and the foundation of a new movement which would clear out this accumulation of unacceptables was not an unattractive idea.

Other unattractive elements had been hovering on the political firmament. One of the most pressing was the issue of the Boundary Commission. Article 12 of the Treaty – the one which

Lord Birkenhead saw as its most essential – was the one under which a commission was to establish the limits of the jurisdiction of the Belfast Parliament. Rumours about the Boundary Commission, circulated in the British press, were strengthening the resolve of Lemass and de Valera to enter the Free State parliament. Eoin MacNeill resigned as the Free State representative on the Commission and the Irish government entered into an agreement with London that the boundary remain unaltered. De Valera issued the following statement:

> When Eoin MacNeill resigned I had hoped that no Irishman, North or South, would be prepared to put his hand to an instrument dismembering his country; but now that such Irishmen have been found my only hope is that the people will not consent to it.

De Valera and his republican TDs, including Lemass, met on 7 December at a meeting called by the Labour leader in the Shelbourne Hotel. It failed to achieve anything on the boundary question, but by now it was clear to those who met there, that the policy of abstention was a futile exercise.

Therefore the formation of a new party was not the major surprise de Valera later suggested it was. Lemass had seen the writing on the wall for Sinn Féin for some time. De Valera said he was considering quitting public life. He later claimed that he was dissuaded from this course of action by Lemass:

> On that day in March 1926, I happened to be walking out of the Rathmines Town Hall with Seán Lemass. I had just resigned as president of Sinn Féin and I said to him, 'Well Seán, I have done my best, but I have been beaten. Now this is the end for me. I am leaving public life.' Seán was shocked to hear me saying this, and he said: 'But you are not going to leave us now Dev, at this stage...we must form a new organisation...it is the only way forward.' We discussed it further and at last I told him I could not but agree with his logic and said I would do all the necessary things.

The new movement was under way. It had in effect been underway since December 1922, the darkest hour of the Civil War. Many years later, when he was President of Ireland, De Valera described to Michael McInerney of *The Irish Times* how he had told friends at that time that 'no matter what way the fighting went there would have to be a political solution ultimately, and a political organisation would be needed'. De Valera announced the notion with customary certitude and by 1926 it was coming to pass.

3

FOUNDING THE WARRIORS OF DESTINY

On Good Friday 1926 Lemass assembled a group of de Valera supporters in the old Sinn Féin headquarters at 23 Suffolk Street. The purpose of the meeting was to lay the groundwork for de Valera's 'new organisation'. Its formal launch would be elsewhere. Lemass had already been party to a series of meetings held in de Valera's house in Serpentine Avenue, Sandymount, in the wake of the Sinn Féin split. The men who met there were of a like cast of mind; they were the new breed of republican realists who, like Lemass, had grown weary not just of the Father O'Flanagan school of romantic republicanism but also of the more militant variety. De Valera called them the 'old team'. Amongst them was Seán T. O'Kelly, Frank Aiken, Gerry Boland, Seán MacEntee and P.J. Ruttledge; men who would form the core of the new party's hierarchy.

Few Irish organisations seem to enter this world without the benefit of a good row and in this regard Fianna Fáil was no exception. The first disagreement was over the party's name. Lemass wished it to be called simply the Republican Party. De Valera wanted a name which would symbolise the spirit of the ancient Fianna, which in turn would be a symbol of the banding together of the Irish people, as he saw it, for service in a 'national movement'. The term national movement soon found ready currency as a description for Fianna Fáil. Lemass had no difficulty with the concept of the party as a national movement, indeed in his travels around Ireland he did much to encourage the notion, but he feared that the Gaelic name would be misunderstood or indeed worse still misinterpreted. De Valera was rather pleased in an impish, scholarly way that the name would not translate too easily into English. Lemass was more concerned that the Irish word 'fáil' would be read as the English word 'fail'. After the oracles, in the form of An tAthair Peadar O'Laoghaire and The O'Rahilly, were consulted, a compromise was agreed and the name Fianna Fáil (The Republican Party) was settled on. Dr Ronan Fanning has observed that the simple truth, explicit in the name de Valera had chosen, was that by implication it was 'the most nationalist, the most anti-British and most quintessentially Irish of all Irish parliamentary parties'.

When Fianna Fáil or the Warriors or Soldiers of Destiny was founded Seán Lemass was just two months short of his twenty-seventh birthday.

The Boundary Commission débâcle lost the Free State government some of its supporters who went on to found a new party, Clann Éireann. It was rumoured that de Valera, Lemass and others would join with them. On 13 April 1926 de Valera moved to quash the speculation:

> The fact is the we are ourselves forming a new organisation....We are convinced that the ideal of the majority is still broadly the Republican ideal – an Ireland united, free and Irish – and that the people can be banded together for the pursuit of that ideal if a reasonable programme based on the existing conditions be set before them. We intend at any rate to make trial and see.

Four days later, on 17 April, de Valera used the opportunity of an interview with a correspondent from the United Press news agency to tell not just the whole of Ireland and Europe but especially the United States of America the aims and objectives of the new party:

> The new Republican organisation, Fianna Fáil, has for its purpose the re-uniting of the Irish people and the banding of them together for the tenacious pursuit of the following ultimate aims, using at every moment such means as are rightly available.
> 1. Securing the political independence of a united Ireland as a Republic.

2. The restoration of the Irish language, and the development of a native Irish culture.
3. The development of a social system in which, as far as possible, equal opportunity will be afforded to every Irish citizen to live a noble and useful Christian life.
4. The distribution of the land of Ireland so as to get the greatest number possible rooted in the soil of Ireland.
5. The making of Ireland an economic unit, as self-contained and self-sufficient as possible, with a proper balance between agriculture and other essential industries.

De Valera put on record the removal of the oath as the immediate political objective of the new party. He described the oath as being posed as a political test on all who would become members of the Free State parliament. The oath, he said, was the primary barrier to national unity and no republican would take it, as it implied England's right to the 'overlordship' of Ireland.

The stage was now set for the launch of the party and a particularly dramatic stage was chosen – that of the La Scala theatre in Prince's Street, later the Capitol cinema. On 16 May the initiates gathered within a biscuit's throw of the General Post Office to hear the creed of the new organisation proclaimed. De Valera wasted no time in addressing the question of the oath of allegiance:

> For me, it is enough that it is called an 'oath' officially and that it begins with 'I do solemnly swear' and whenever it suits it will be held to be an oath by those who impose it and will be so understood by the world. I say if it is not an oath why not do away with the mockery? Why not end the whole of this abominable prevarication at once? Why retain it as an instrument for our national and moral degradation and set it as a headline for lying and perjury for the whole country?

Lemass was keen that what was launched in La Scala should be a movement of substance. For that end both he and de Valera were anxious to embrace as many elements of the republican movement as was possible. Lemass's sense of *realpolitik* had developed sufficiently by early 1926 for him to articulate what remained unsaid about rump Sinn Féin:

> Sinn Féin, for good or ill, is entering on another stage in its career...there are some who would have us sit by the roadside and debate abstruse points about a *de jure* this and a *de facto* that, but the reality we want is away in the distance – and we cannot get there unless we move.

Lemass knew that in the break with Sinn Féin he and de Valera had left behind the elements they had wished to shed but it was clear from de Valera's opening speech at La Scala that the new movement would be recruiting from the ranks of their old IRA comrades. Lemass had made a nation-wide peregrination rallying the troops to the flag of the new movement. In *The Party : Inside Fianna Fáil*, Dick Walsh says those who answered the call along with the veterans were 'the supporters of Gaelic games and the speakers of Gaelic, the teachers, small farmers and farm labourers, many of them, de Valera remarked, from the poorest sections of the community'.

Neal Blaney, father of Neil T. Blaney TD, was one such early recruit enlisted by Lemass. Neil Blaney recalled the meeting:

> My father and Lemass were not meeting for the first time. I recollect that my father also knew Lemass's brother Noel. As a child I recall the arrival of a motorcar in our area was still something of a novelty. Lemass got out of the car and made his way to the field where my father was saving hay. I still remember this impressive man wearing a cap and walking, what I considered to be the long way round, to where my father was working. He never discussed with me what he and Lemass talked about.

Blaney senior was not easily won over but by the time Lemass had left him he had agreed to be a Fianna Fáil candidate in Donegal. Many years later, when driving in Donegal, Lemass pointed to a field and told his daughter Peggy, 'That's the spot where Fianna Fáil was founded in Donegal'.

De Valera and Lemass also brought with them into Fianna Fail several influential women, amongst them, Countess Markievicz, Mrs Tom Clarke, Mrs Pearse and Miss Margaret Pearse.

On the eve of the La Scala meeting there had been a successful IRA jailbreak which secured the release of the popular and prominent republican, Jack Keogh. De Valera did a warm-up of his audience with a reference to the Keogh release. He suggested that Fianna Fáil should apply the same meticulous preparation to the political task which faced it, as the liberators of Jack Keogh had done when facing their task. The opening gambit worked like a treat and from there on de Valera had the crowd in his hands.

What, he asked his audience, would a young Irishman with 'strong national feelings' see when he pondered on the contemporary political scene? He told them such a young man would see the country partitioned and nearly half of the electorate shut out from having an effective voice in determining its rulers. Tracing that anomaly to its source, should pose that hypothetical young Irishman no great difficulty, de Valera said. If he wished to source it he need only look to the oath of allegiance to a foreign power, agreed to by the majority under threat of war. What was in place in 1926, he said, was a pretence at democracy.

The oath of allegiance was isolated and held up to a degree of odium on a par only with the oath of supremacy. De Valera said as much in a speech to his Clare constituents on 29 June 1926. For Fianna Fáil the abolition of the oath became an article of faith, for it was, in the founder's words 'a denial of national faith' which had to be smashed.

The faithful who left the La Scala theatre did so, in Kevin Boland's words, 'to light the flame in their own parishes and pave the way for the writing of Emmet's epitaph'.

For the La Scala delegates the tablet on which that epitaph might yet be etched was in the safekeeping of de Valera. But for de Valera the principal issue that might allow the composition of that epitaph – a solution to partition – was sidelined with singular skill and, for the moment, he concentrated on the single issue of the oath.

Lemass was confident that with de Valera as leader they would soon have a nationwide organisation. On the 24 November, the anniversary of the execution of Erskine Childers, the first Fianna Fáil Árd Fheis took place. In the intervening six months Lemass and Gerry Boland masterminded the establishment of cumainn [branches] right across the country. Lemass's pragmatic approach to the structuring of the party organisation was uniquely stamped on Fianna Fáil in those first six months. He was faced with an extremely difficult task. He had insufficient funds; initially the use of one Baby Austin motorcar (later he scraped together £25 to purchase five others), a secretary in Dublin and very little else save exceptional determination. Professor John A. Murphy has pointed out that there has been a tendency to underplay de Valera's role in the organisational work in those early days. While Boland and Lemass were in one part of the country de Valera and Tommy Mullins, the party's first General Secretary, were often in another. They travelled over 1,500 miles in west Cork alone in the effort to establish 45 cumainn there. An official history of the party, for which Lemass wrote a preface in 1960, tells us that the party's first headquarters was at 35 Lower O'Connell Street, opposite and looking down on the General Post Office. Its furnishings were scant and its finances came principally from friends and chapel-gate collections – a device which Lemass hailed as the best barometer of public support for the party.

As the Árd Fheis opened in Dublin's Rotunda, Lemass was concerned about the danger of the renewal of the Civil War. His fears were echoed in de Valera's speech to the Árd Fheis:

It is vain to think that the natural aspirations of Irishmen for the liberty of their country are going to be stifled now. If the road of peaceful progress and natural evolution be barred, then the road of revolution will beckon and will be taken. Positive law and natural right will be involved in the old conflict. The question of majority rule and minority right will again be bloodily fought out, and when the fight is over it will probably be found out once more that the problem has remained and that force is not the solution.

That first Árd Fheis passed a raft of resolutions asserting the unity and sovereignty of the Irish nation; it called for the restoration of the Irish language, the introduction of protectionist tariffs and for the establishment of a state bank and credit system.

'One movement, two groups' was how *An Phoblacht* was describing the relationship between Fianna Fáil and Sinn Féin in the period around the new party's first Árd Fheis. Fianna Fail meetings and events were given prominent notice in its pages and its editorials took a concilliatory stand towards de Valera and his party. Lemass told Michael Mills of the *Irish Press* he was surprised, as he travelled around Ireland organising Fianna Fáil cumainn, to find that the republicans he was targeting for support were not divided along the lines that the Sinn Féin Árd Fheis, at which the split occurred, seemed to suggest. He told Michael Mills:

> Within a year of the first Fianna Fáil executive being set up, we had a nationwide organisation, the strongest in the country, fully geared for action with cumainn and county executives everywhere. The speed with which the Fianna Fáil organisation, came into being, from a group sitting in Dublin to a nationwide organisation extending to every parish in the country was quite phenomenal.

Lemass has been given due credit for the speed with which the party took root in the provinces. He has been described by T.P. O'Neill as 'the driving genius' behind Fianna Fáil's successful organisational and disciplined structure. Every free moment was spent travelling the length and breadth of the country in battered Fords convincing and cajoling Sinn Féin and IRA supporters that their future lay with Fianna Fáil. He brought Fianna Fáil's populist and republican policies to workers, small farmers and nationalists as he espoused economic self-sufficiency and highlighted the negative aspects of the Cosgrave administration's policies. This work took its toll on his family life, keeping him away from home several nights a week and most weekends, until the demands of ministerial office saw him withdraw more and more from the role of party organiser. Since Fianna Fáil had very little money – until de Valera's fund raising efforts in the United States began to pay off – Lemass was still dependant on his father for an income to support his family. Though he had severed his link with the Capel Street shop Lemass continued to be financially dependant on his father until he took his seat in the Dáil in 1927.

That year saw two general elections held in Ireland in June and in September.

With de Valera in America for the early part of 1927 it was left to Lemass and a handful of his colleagues to ensure that Fianna Fáil was ready for its first electoral test. There was speculation in the press and in political circles of possible alliances between Fianna Fáil and various groups, including Clann Eireann and the IRA. A meeting which Lemass had with Peadar O'Donnell put an end to speculation about the latter alliance. Such an alliance would have weakened Fianna Fáil's credibility as an independent political party, though as we shall see later, Lemass did much to keep the lines of communication between Fianna Fáil and the IRA open. It seems unlikely that there was any truth in the speculation about an alliance with Clann Éireann, established as a party, as a result of the Boundary Commission fall-out in Cumann na nGaedheal. The Clann was led by Professor William Magennis, a National University TD, once described as 'a windbag with a nasty streak of malice'. Fianna Fáil had little in common with the men who led this curious band of Christian crusaders and protectionists, though Dan Breen, elected as a Republican TD in 1923, had a brief flirtation with the party. Fianna Fáil decided to face the electorate on its own.

It fielded 87 candidates for the 153 Dáil seats in all constituencies except the universities and North Cork. For the election the party employed the slogan 'Fianna Fáil is going in'. There was however, no clear commitment, at this stage, that this meant the party would take up its seats in the Dáil. Not a few members of the Roman Catholic clergy pointed this fact out to their congregations, condemning Fianna Fáil as a group of abstentionist anarchists.

Lemass was principally responsible for the Dublin constituencies where he romped home heading the poll and with more than 300 votes ahead of the nearest rival. The party won 26.1 per cent of the first preference vote and while that was a percentage point down on the performance of Sinn Féin in 1923 it secured the same number of seats, 44. Sinn Féin, which made clear its abstentionist policy, secured only 3.6 per cent of the votes and 5 seats. That part of the electorate which was firmly anti-Treaty was no longer voting for those who touted the purist republican line.

For Cumann na nGaedheal the election result came as a severe blow. In the 1923 election it had secured 63 seats, now it won but 46. With the support of the Ceann Comhairle, something it would soon need, the party had 47 seats in the 153 seater Dáil. Two Independent Republicans were returned, one of whom joined Fianna Fáil. Labour took 22 seats, there were 14 Independents, 11 Farmers and 8 National League members.

After the inconclusive result Fianna Fáil now turned the full focus of its gaze to the question of the oath. Its view was that if a referendum on the issue was held the oath would go. De Valera made this statement on the matter of the oath to the New York Tribune:

We intend to claim out seats and to exercise our right to represent our constituents without submitting to an oath of

43

allegiance to any foreign power. If excluded from the assembly by force, it will be at the insistance of a party whose strength is less than one third of the whole elected body. If not thus excluded, we believe we can form a strong national government with the support of all the progressive non-imperalist elements.

The party took legal advice on the question of the oath and was told there was no authority for excluding any deputy, whether he had taken the oath or not, before the House was duly constituted and the Ceann Comhairle elected. When de Valera and his party presented this argument to the Clerk of the Dáil on 23 June it failed to impress him. On refusing to sign what the Clerk called the 'little formality' the deputies were turned away. Rejection, which they knew to be inevitable, afforded Fianna Fáil a brilliant publicity coup.

Backed by the Fianna Fáil National Executive Lemass and Seán T. O'Kelly then lent their names to a legal action which challenged the validity of the oath on the basis of opinion proffered by counsel. At the same time a petition under Article 48 of the Constitution was proposed by de Valera. That article made provision for a referendum upon receipt of the signatures of 75,000 voters. Events soon intervened to make both Lemass's legal action and the petition redundant.

On Sunday 10 July, Kevin O'Higgins, who combined the portfolios of Minister for Justice and Minister for External Affairs in Cosgrave's cabinet, as well as being Cosgrave's vice-president, made his way from his Blackrock home to attend mass. As he did so he was shot by three gunmen. He was hit seven times and died some hours after being found by Eoin MacNeill.

The government reacted to the O'Higgins murder with three pieces of legislation, two of which had serious consequences for Fianna Fáil. The first was a Public Safety Bill which gave the government extraordinary powers against organisations it considered seditious. The second was an Electoral Amendment Bill which hit at the very root of what Fianna Fáil were trying to do with the oath. It required every candidate for election to Dáil

Eireann to sign, on nomination, an affidavit, that if elected he would take his seat and the oath of allegiance within two months of election. Failure to do so lost the elected candidate his seat. The third measure abolished the provision in the Constitution which allowed the people to petition for a referendum.

The gates of Leinster House now seemed more firmly shut than ever in the face of Fianna Fáil. In late July and in August Fianna Fáil had a series of meetings with Labour and the National League but in the end nothing substantial came of the notion of an alliance. Dan Breen had taken the oath and he was followed on 26 July by Patrick Belton. Now, as before, Lemass had decided to stand by de Valera's decision, whatever that might be. However, he warned that it was now clear that other Fianna Fáil TDs might take the same action as Belton and the party would be left as a spent force. It was also clear that the policy of abstention exacerbated political unrest and that the country was again becoming polarised along the old lines of division.

Tim Pat Coogan says de Valera's decision to take the oath and enter the Dáil was a situation where, '...ever a man to share responsibility, if not authority, he ensured that as many as possible of his party were involved in the decision'.

The National Executive met on 9 August and the Fianna Fáil TDs on the following evening. De Valera made it clear to both meetings that he would lead the party into the Dáil. A statement was issued which gave Irish politics one of its most immortal phrases when de Valera described the oath as 'an empty formality':

> ...so that there be no doubt as to their attitude, and and no misunderstanding of their action, the Fianna Fáil deputies hereby give public notice that they intend to regard the declaration as an empty formality and repeat that their own allegiance is to the Irish nation, and that it will be given to no other power or authority.

On 11 August de Valera led his party into Leinster House to sign the 'empty formality'. The way in which he did it has been much written about. He covered the oath with some papers he was carrying, removed a Bible to one corner of the room and uttered the phrase to the Clerk of the Dáil 'I want you to understand I am not taking any oath nor giving any promise of faithfulness to the King of England...'. His deputies, Lemass included, followed his example and a new era in Irish politics was born. Its birth came as a surprise to some and a shock to others. Bertie Smylie, the editor of *The Irish Times*, said W.T. Cosgrave was shocked when he told him 'Dev is going in'.

An Phoblacht denounced Fianna Fáil for its decision; some members including Hanna Sheehy-Skeffington resigned. On 16 August Labour tabled a vote of no confidence in the government. De Valera agreed to back a coalition of Labour and the National League. His calculations showed him that they would have a majority of three votes over Cumann na nGaedheal and its satellite supporters. That majority was reduced with the decision of Vincent Rice of Redmond's National League not to support the pact. It was further reduced in an almost farcical manner when another National League deputy John Jinks of Sligo was plied with drink by ex-Unionist Bryan Cooper, an inveterate boozer, and Bertie Smylie also renowned for his fondness of the 'odd drop'. They convinced the hapless Jinks that the best interests of the Sligo ex-servicemen who returned him to Dáil Éireann, would not be served by putting Fianna Fáil in power. Jinks turned tail and took the train back to Sligo.

When the confidence vote was called it resulted in a tie. The government survived only with the casting vote of the Ceann Comhairle. However its success in two by-elections prompted W.T. Cosgrave to call a snap general election for 15 September.

All parties suffered from a lack of funds but Fianna Fáil had its American support to fall back on. Lemass made moves to canvass support from what remained of Clann Éireann and he actively canvassed votes from Labour supporters for Fianna Fáil candidates. It was Lemass's grasp of the importance of the techniques of mass organisation and his use of newspaper advertising for the campaign, as well as the more traditional electioneering methods, which helped secure Fianna Fáil 57 seats. Fianna Fáil and the government gained at the expense of the smaller parties. The National League was reduced to 2 deputies and Labour took only 13 seats, losing 9 deputies including party leader Thomas Johnson. Cumann na nGaedheal won 62 seats, Independents 12, the Farmers Party 6 and the other seat went to an Independent Labour candidate. In his own constituency Lemass came in head of the poll increasing his vote by over 2,700 votes.

Over the next five years Lemass set about the task of learning the art and craft of the parliamentarian.

4

A SLIGHTLY CONSTITUTIONAL PARTY

'I think you will find the average age amongst all parties is just over thirty. In the Cumann na nGaedheal Party it is much higher, because, after all, that is the party that would naturally attract those suffering from senile decay, whereas young and vigorous men would be attracted by the policy of Fianna Fáil....If you wish to have a useful institution in your Second Chamber you should decide that only those should be elected as Senators who are under six or over sixty.'

The voice is that of a young TD who was cutting his parliamentary teeth, just one year after entering Dáil Éireann, and using them skillfully in debates in the House.

The tone of the remark was uncharacteristic for even his political opponents acknowledged that, almost alone amongst his contemporaries, Seán Lemass did not trade in the bitter rhetoric of political insult in debates inside or outside the House. The Minister for Justice, J. Fitzgerald-Kenney, said of him that he delivered his remarks in the Dáil without the 'conscious giving of offence to anyone'. W.T. Cosgrave remarked on the fine spirit with which Lemass addressed himself to the controversial debate on the Public Safety (Repeal) Bill and the deputy himself reminded the House of his temperate nature in April 1930, when he said it was not usual for him to make personal reference to anyone. Within two months of making that remark he delivered one of the few exceptions to that rule when he made a bitter attack on SeánMacEoin on 18 June 1930. He shouted across the floor of the house: 'On your soul lies the crime of murder.'

In his first year in the Dáil Lemass spent a great deal of time pursuing the Minister for Justice on cases concerning alleged intimidation of republicans by the Gárdaí. On 11 November 1928 he raised the matter of the president, secretary and treasurer of Drogheda Fianna Fáil cumann whose houses were raided for arms and whose correspondence from party headquarters was examined by the Gárdaí. Such enquiries by Lemass became routine and he rarely received much satisfaction by way of assurances from the Minister on the questions he raised about the raids. Though on one occasion the Minister for Justice gave credit to Lemass as an 'astute debater' when putting his case on behalf of a County Leitrim man who claimed Gárda intimidation. The cases raised often illustrated the close association between Fianna Fáil and the IRA, the nature of which is discussed below.

On 30 November 1928, speaking on the Adjournment Debate, he asked that if the House was going into recess for three months would the Civic Guard continue its policy of raids on Fianna Fáil members' homes. He said:

It is not their duty to raid the houses of members of the Fianna Fáil organisation and to read the communications I send to the various secretaries through the country. If the Minister wants to know what Fianna Fáil is doing I will arrange with the editor of *The Nation* to send him a copy of that paper, free of charge, every week, and he will be able to keep himself fully informed as to the activities and the growing strength of the organisation...

Lemass is often portrayed as being obsessed with the organisation of the party in its early years. However, he did not restrict his activities to the organisational side of the party machine. He began to put to effective use the vast amount of knowledge he had acquired from his reading of economic theory.

On 26 October 1927 Lemass made one of his earliest references in the House to a policy with which he would become closely associated – protection. The Labour party introduced a Dáil motion on the relief of unemployment. Lemass blamed the unemployment problem on the financial system operated by the Government and he called for emergency measures to be put in place. He said a policy of protection was the 'key to the whole situation'. The protection of Irish industry would make it more profitable for the investment of Irish capital.

His preference for a policy of state intervention, such as was in operation in other European states, became clear when he spoke in the House in February 1928:

> We consider that the entire economic policy of the country should be decided on by a national economic council such as exists in Germany and France and such as is suggested by one of the big English parties of that nation....Until we get a definite national policy decided on in favour of industrial and agricultural protection and an executive in office prepared to enforce that policy, it is useless to hope for results.

He went on in that speech to indicate that what he favoured was not the operation of economic policy to benefit one class or another but a symbiosis of economic and social policy to benefit all.

More than one observer has noted the influence of Arthur Griffith's thinking on the development of Lemass's economic policies. The distinguished economist, Professor Patrick Lynch, has remarked that it is a nice historical irony, at which, as dialecticians, Marx and Engels would have smiled, that Griffith's protectionist policy for industrialisation had to wait implementation until Lemass took control of the Irish economy.

Lemass favoured a programme of rapid industrialisation but before assuming office he had no doctrinaire economic position; however, his stated preference for state intervention in economic matters gave a somewhat leftward direction to his economic policies after 1932. He attacked the government for its lack of an industrialised economic ideology. He said '...a country in which over-production is a disaster and in which unemployment and poverty can exist side by side, has some serious defects in its economic organisation'.

His advocacy of the development of private enterprise by protectionist policies was tempered with an awareness of the limitations of the doctrine. He was against outright monopoly yet

50

vigorous in his defence of state intervention; particularly in the running of the national rail network and a nationalised system of car insurance.

Before Fianna Fáil took office, and for some time after, the mind of the civil service was closed to all but the British liberal and *laissez-faire* tradition. Lemass criticised this trend saying that the inherited administrative system left much to be desired when it came to the organisation of the economy.

Lemass has been credited as being the architect of Fianna Fáil's first published economy policy document, and though it appeared to be essentially a rehash of a Dáil speech delivered by de Valera, what the 1928 paper really reflected was Lemass's thinking on economic self-sufficiency and industrial growth.

However, an economic policy document Lemass prepared for presentation to the party in July 1929 contained more of his own original thinking. It strongly advocated a protectionist policy without giving any credence to the notion that such a policy might lead to prices rises for the Irish consumer. It was also strongly anti-foreign capital in tone:

> In the first place those who control industry can exercise a considerable influence on the determination of national policy...they will undoubtedly render it difficult to adopt measures designed to protect national interests when those interests are in conflict with their own....There have been many examples in recent years of countries which permitted foreign capital to get too strong a grip on their resources.

As the country edged closer to a general election Lemass's speeches began to reflect more and more his penchant for wanting to marry economic and social policy for the benefit of all the community. This was evident when he spoke in the 1930 Budget debate:

> ...I say the first concerns of this Dáil should be to protect the interests and preserve the happiness of the men who build up the wealth of the country, and they are not dukes, earls or

millionaires. They are plain, good, honest-to-God, working men whose interests were neglected when this Budget was framed.

Professor Brian Farrell notes there were 'considerable elements of political calculation' in Lemass's parliamentary rhetoric in his early years in the Dáil. He observes that 'There was a sustained effort to score off a government that "has been driving the industrial car with its foot on the brake instead of on the accelerator", and that had, in Lemass's view, no positive policy to offer.'

Lemass directed his attention to policy areas other than the economic. He pointed out to de Valera something his leader was already aware of, namely that they lacked support in one very obvious and important area – amongst the Catholic hierarchy. At the foundation of the party not one senior bishop could be termed a supporter of Fianna Fáil. Indeed the reverse of the medal was the case.

'Plunder, devastation and ruin' is how one County Galway cleric described Fianna Fáil policy in 1927. To vote for Fianna Fáil a County Clare parish priest told the faithful was to 'hand over the country to be destroyed by the destroyers'.

In the early years of its Dáil performance Fianna Fáil wasted no time in attempting to win favour with the Roman Catholic Church. Those who had been served with the writ of excommunication could be heard berating the government for the appointment of a Protestant librarian in County Mayo, a Protestant postmistress here or a Protestant dispensary doctor elsewhere. Cumann na nGaedheal resisted such Opposition objections, as it did Seán T. O'Kelly's bid to have prayers said before the commencement of Dáil business and a ban put on its meeting on holy days of obligation. However, W.T. Cosgrave was a devout Roman Catholic. He had proposed to de Valera in February 1921 that there should be a sort of Upper House to the Dáil consisting of a 'theological board which would decide if any enactments of the Dáil were contrary to faith and morals or not'.

It is not surprising that the civil service advised against such a notion. Nor did anything come of Cosgrave's plan to give the site of the GPO to the Archdiocese of Dublin for the building of a cathedral. But as John Cooney, in his book *The Crozier and the Dáil: Church and State 1922-1986* observes:

> If such pious schemes failed to materialise, the new State had little hesitation in accepting and enforcing Catholic teaching on matters such as divorce and contraception and used censorship to cultivate a closed society, reinforced by strong Church control of the educational system...

Fianna Fáil followed the direction taken by the Cosgrave administration on church-state relations but for Fianna Fáil the Church proved no easy target for wooing. It was suspicious of the party's promise to extend the social welfare system and as it faced into the 1932 general election, not a few churchmen could still be heard warning their congregations that Fianna Fáil's social policies amounted to little more than outright communism.

The anti-clerical republicans in the Civil War rejected only the Church's competence to pronounce on political matters. Lemass could be counted among their number. They had no argument with the priests over matters of moral teaching and were therefore not anti-clerical in the continental manner. Peadar O'Donnell remarked that Ireland was 'not a cleric ridden country, it is a yahoo ridden Church'.

Lemass had no difficulty supporting O'Kelly's wish for prayers before Dáil business or with Fianna Fáil's almost comical rush to denounce Cumann na nGaedheal as lackeys for the Freemasons. He was pragmatic enough to reconcile even that absurd claim, and his party's self-imposed pietism, with its need to reach a *modus vivendi* with the Catholic hierarchy before the 1932 general election. History may look less kindly on his support for the Censorship of Publications Bill in 1929 and a Legitimacy Bill of the following year which conformed to Vatican teaching.

Lemass and de Valera were seeking to outflank W.T. Cosgrave in a bid to secure clerical support. They were urged by churchmen like Monsignor John Hagan of the Irish College in Rome to waste no time in becoming respectable in the eyes of Mother Church. Fianna Fáil may have been founded in the La Scala theatre but so influential was the outcome of Hagan's advice that it prompted Dr Dermot Keogh to write in his book, *The Vatican, the Bishops and Irish Politics, 1919-39*, that 'it can be argued that the decision to found Fianna Fáil was probably taken in the Irish College in Rome'.

In 1929 it fell to Seán T. O'Kelly – by then the arbiter of all that was Catholic in Fianna Fáil – to hail it as Ireland's Catholic party:

> We of the Fianna Fáil party believe that we speak for the big body of Catholic opinion. I think I could say, without qualifications of any kind, that we represent the big body of Catholicity.

More secular elements had to be wooed as well.

It fell to Lemass principally to keep the lines of communication with the IRA open. Such support as might be had from the IRA would be of considerable advantage to Fianna Fáil as it faced into the 1932 campaign. The party's opposition to repressive security measures was aimed at winning republican support as was the play on the partition question. Fianna Fáil presented itself as the party of a united Ireland and as soon as it had taken up its seats in the Dáil it set about placing on the record of the House that it blamed the British and Free State governments for partition.

There was no need for the party to sever its links with the IRA at this stage – that would come later. John A. Murphy has pointed out that Fianna Fáil and the IRA had a common socio-political background and ultimately a common objective. Not all elements of the IRA leadership were aware of just how much of a constitutional party Fianna Fáil had become, within the framework of the Free State legislature, which the IRA leadership so very much despised.

Lemass's now famous declaration of Fianna Fáil as a 'slightly constitutional party' though made in the heat of parliamentary debate, has been seen as an attempt to win support from the harder-edged republicans who had little time for conventional constitutional parties. Fianna Fáil's apparent readiness to 'go outside the system' if constitutional methods failed, secured some republican support but it did not convince those republicans who had no time for any form of constitutional politics.

Lemass's remark was off the cuff and made during a sometimes heated debate in Private Members' time on the regulations governing the treatment of political prisoners. Fianna Fáil proposed that the government establish a Select Committee to review the cases of all prisoners who claimed that their position arose out of the Civil War. The aim of the debate was to focus attention on the government's hardline law and order attitude on the subject. William Davin, Labour TD for Leix-Offaly, supported the Fianna Fáil proposal but concluded his remarks rather curiously by saying he did so in the hope of learning the real meaning of constitutional activity as interpreted by Fianna Fáil. This provoked the following from Lemass:

> I think it would be right to inform Deputy Davin that Fianna Fáil is a slightly constitutional party. We are perhaps open to the definition of a constitutional party, but, before anything, we are a republican party. We have adopted the method of political agitation to achieve our end, because we believe, in the present circumstances, that method is best in the interests of the nation, and of the republican movement, and for no other reason.

At this point the South Mayo TD, T.J. O'Connell, interjected to say 'It took you five years to make up your mind.' Lemass retorted:

> Five years ago the methods we adopted were not the methods we have adopted now. Five years ago, we were on the defensive; perhaps in time we may recoup our strength sufficiently to go on the offensive. Our objective is to establish a republican government in Ireland. If that can be done by the present methods we have, we will be very pleased, but, if not, we would not confine ourselves to them.

The remarks were intemperate and made in the heat of debate. There is little evidence to suggest that Lemass was less than wholeheartedly dedicated to the democratic process by this time and while he may have been keeping an eye on republican support, it is unlikely that this outburst was aimed specifically in that direction.

Lemass had crossed swords in the House with Deputy Davin on a previous occasion when he annoyed the Leix-Offaly member by suggesting that Labour's 'invertebrate attitude' had been the product of its 'long association with this House'. A still inexperienced parliamentarian made the 'slightly constitutional' remark thereby saying perhaps a great deal more than he meant. Brian Farrell has given by far the most convincing explanation of the remark:

> ...he blurted out some of the residual frustration of a defeated armed militancy which, at a considered level, he had already abandoned. Certainly his own gloss on the remark in the Dáil a month later presents Lemass as an essentially constitutional parliamentary politician.

He was speaking on that occasion on a Fianna Fáil motion to remove the oath of allegiance. He offered the view that the government's attitude to the Constitution as an 'intolerable nuisance' was not wholly different from Fianna Fáil's and that their attitude had shown them to be 'only slightly constitutional as well'.

Lemass received no flack from the party leadership after his memorable addition to the political lexicon. Such flack was unlikely to come from de Valera. His own utterances seemed to indicate that he too seemed confused as to just how constitutional a party Fianna Fáil really was in those early opposition years.

In 1926, nearly two years before Lemass made his remark in the Dáil, de Valera had told the first Árd Fheis that if the path of peaceful progress were barred 'the road of revolution will beckon and will be taken'. But to confuse the issue further he told the electorate in 1927:

We shall proceed as a responsible constitutional government acknowledging without reserve that all authority comes through the sovereign people and that, and before any important step likely to involve their safety is taken, the people are entitled to be taken into the fullest consultation.

What was clear, in 1928, is that Lemass was following de Valera's lead down the road of Machiavellian sophistry to produce a somewhat confused end-product when it came to defining his party's relationship to constitutional politics. It was an end-product which helped prompt National University member Patrick McGilligan to say in the Dáil that there were two Lemasses, the 'responsible economist' and the 'irreconcilable militant'. There was more than a grain of truth in McGilligan's description.

That Lemass was becoming a responsible economist and constitutional republican was increasingly evident from his contributions to debates in Leinster House. That he was prepared to see the civil liberties of those whose republicanism was more militant safeguarded, was also evident from those speeches. But there remained for some time to come a degree of ambiguity surrounding his attitude to IRA violence. Nowhere was that more evident than when he told Peadar O'Donnell 'Don't you see that we stand to gain from your organisation so long as we can't be accused of starting the turmoil?'

By the beginning of 1930 the Government was alarmed at the increase in IRA activity across the country. Few arms of government was more alarmed that the Special Branch. Lemass thought that the increase in activity was being met with, at times, unnecessarily repressive measures.

By 1931 the courts of justice were no longer capable of dealing with the campaign unleashed by the IRA. Jurors were intimidated, the Gárdaí were being attacked, informers and policemen were being killed. *An Phoblacht* urged that members of the CID should be treated like 'social pariahs'. The Department of Justice advised Mr Cosgrave to reintroduce the military tribunal. In setting up the tribunal Cosgrave gave a warning that would have implications for Fianna Fáil a little bit further down the road. He said it was necessary not just for his government but may well be necessary for future governments.

The IRA and several left-wing organisations were declared unlawful in October 1931.

It was a time when the Special Branch was obsessed with what it saw as the 'red scare'. It began to see communism everywhere; in Cumann na mBann, in the IRA Army Council, in tenant's rights committees and in Fianna Fáil. One Special Branch report claimed that Frank Aiken and Robert Briscoe (named as 'Briscoe the Jew') were closely associated with the Communists. Fianna Fáil would not itself be beyond spreading rumours of the 'red scare' in later years but for the moment Lemass was more concerned with the government's attitude to the IRA. He put it thus in the Dáil in 1931:

> There is a situation which concerns all of us.... We think that the Dáil, before arming itself with jackboots to deal with these people, many of whom, however mistaken they are, hold their convictions quite sincerely, should examine that method.

Such statements, made in what the IRA still called the 'usurping legislature', paid dividends for Fianna Fáil in the 1932 general election. Speaking on a Constitutional Amendment on the reform of the Senate on 5 July 1928 Lemass made a strong attack on the descendants of the landlord class who he said were now being placed by the government in a power position in the Senate. They were words that would have found a great deal of sympathy with republicans:

> For the past fifty years the Irish people have been striving to shake off the grip upon this country which was maintained by the descendants of the Plantation soldiery of Cromwell. For fifty years the Irish people have been trying to make good their authority in this country. For fifty years they have been trying to put into the hands of the Irish people the economic resources of the country. For fifty years they have been trying

to drive out of the national life of Ireland that alien element which was introduced into it by a foreign government and given an unnatural degree of authority. And now at the end of that period and after half a century of struggle during which every conceivable means were used by the Irish people to bring success to their cause – means constitutional and unconstitutional, means vigorous and means timorous, means some of which failed and some of which were successful – after fifty years of such struggle we have a House of Representatives, declaring themselves to be representatives of the Irish people proposing to give back into the hands of that privileged clique the power which the Irish people were endeavouring to take from them.

The maintenance of harmonious relations with the IRA up to that period owed much to Lemass's strategy in raising ill-treatment of prisoners in Dáil debates and to his continuing personal contacts with the IRA leadership.

There were many among the IRA leadership who took the view that they should back Fianna Fáil to put de Valera in and thus get Cosgrave and his law and order hardliners out. Only after the 1932 general election would the IRA begin to see just how constitutional a party Fianna Fáil really had become. It would also see that the allegiance of republican-minded voters had shifted, for the most part, to Fianna Fáil.

5

TOWARDS POWER: 1932

Under the guiding hand of Lemass, Fianna Fáil's election propaganda in 1932 placed considerable emphasis on the need for industrial development in Ireland. The propaganda contrasted the promised land of 'all-round protection' under Fianna Fáil with the emigration boat and declining industry under Cumann na nGaedheal.

Lemass and Gerry Boland commissioned cartoons showing W.T. Cosgrave in the garb of an ascendancy gentleman cavorting with the Freemasons, Unionists, bankers and foreign industrialists but, above all else, with his 'masters' in London. It was not just the newly-founded, de Valera-controlled *Irish Press* in which the cartoons appeared. The merciless cartoonists of the humorous magazine *Dublin Opinion* were no more generous in their portrayal of Mr Cosgrave and his ministers.

Cumann na nGaedheal portrayed Fianna Fáil as Communists whose victory in the election would see land taken from farmers and endanger the stability of the state. A parody of the popular Percy French song which characterised Fianna Fáil as gunmen was widely distributed. Its chorus ran:

'Och! we'll shoot and we'll loot and with bullets we will riddle oh!
We'll keep the whole land sizzling like a herring on the griddle oh!'

The conditions under which Cumann na nGaedheal fought the election were far from auspicious. The Free State had survived the economic collapse of 1929 relatively unscathed. In the years immediately following, the Irish economy was buoyed up by the stable prices of its agricultural exports, whilst also benefiting from a radical drop in the price of imports. On the eve of the 1932 general election Ireland began to suffer the consequences of world recession. Exports declined radically and the government introduced a series of unpopular austerity measures to compensate for the worsening economic climate. Such measures were in keeping with the stern and stoic face which the fathers of the Free State choose to present as their public aspect.

With the establishment of the *Irish Press* Fianna Fáil gained its first real opportunity to put its view of that aspect to a mass audience. Though the name de Valera would dominate the paper from its foundation, Lemass was also closely associated with the newspaper, often directing its use as an instrument of party propaganda and joining the board as managing director in February 1948.

Vol.1 No.1 rolled off the presses on 5 September 1931. To give it an umbilical link to the purest of republican tradition, Patrick Pearse's mother, Margaret, pushed the button which brought the printing-presses to life. Beside her, to give the benediction of Mother Church, was a Carmelite priest; behind her to give overall approval, stood the tall figure of Eamon de Valera.

De Valera believed that the daily press in Ireland was 'consistently pro-British and imperialistic in its outlook'. He invoked the opinion of a prominent Jesuit, Father Devane, to support his view. The distinguished Jesuit had said 'a glance at the counter of any newspaper shop...will convince even the most sceptical that we are in a condition of mental bondage'.

The money for the *Irish Press* was raised principally in Ireland and in the United States through the issue of share capital. The share offer was for 200,000 ordinary shares at £1 each. The board of directors consisted of seven members with de Valera as controlling director with absolute power.

Tim Pat Coogan, a former editor of the newspaper and de Valera's biographer, writes of just how absolute that power was:

He could hire and fire every member of the staff from the copy boy to the managing director. He had authority over every function of the paper from its content to the workings of the circulation department....In addition to being controlling director he could also be editor-in-chief and managing director.

Frank Gallagher, a close associate of de Valera's and a friend of Lemass, was appointed as the first editor of the paper. His prosecution by the government for seditious libel gave Fianna Fáil a welcome publicity coup in the run up to the 1932 general election. Gallagher had published a series of articles and hard-hitting editorials on the ill-treatment of republican prisoners and on prison conditions. The tone of the articles did not fit in with the government's law and order policies and 11 days before polling Gallagher appeared before a military tribunal established under the emergency legislation that contributed so much to Cumann na nGaedheal's unpopularity. Gallagher and the paper were fined £100 each and as a result the paper's circulation rose to an unprecedented 115,000. Polling day was set for 16 February 1932.

Pausing to look at its own achievements, Mr Cosgrave's administration could legitimately boast considerable advances across a whole range of areas. There was substantial postwar reconstruction, a rationalisation of the civil service structure, improvements in agriculture, the development of schemes such as the Shannon hydroelectric system, the introduction of a whole range of progressive legislation, including local government, fisheries, housing, the railways, currency, electricity. All of this was balanced against the ever-present threat of the rekindling of the embers of a civil war in whose wake the government of the Free State ruled.

On the downside was the fact that as the economic depression intensified and the government continued its single-minded application of orthodox economic policies, it saw falling food prices and the value of agricultural exports plummeting. Coupled with this was the inescapable blight of mass emigration and an ever-increasing number of those left behind forced to accept Poor Law assistance.

Cumann na nGaedheal's election manifesto concentrated on its achievements over its ten years in government. It made no mention of one of its more solid achievements – the whole area of external relations – because it appeared tainted, as we shall see later, by association with elements of Commonwealth policy.

Certain measures which formed part of the orthodox housekeeping policies of the Minister for Finance Ernest Blythe, were certain to be of electoral advantage to Fianna Fáil. He proposed cutting pensions for the elderly and the blind, public service paycuts to affect teachers and the police and married women were to be barred from holding teaching posts. Protests came from all quarters. Indeed in 1929 a good indicator of the effects of the government's economic policies could be gauged by the number of motions on economic matters at the IRA's Comhairle na Poblachta Árd Fheis of that year. In other years the programme for debate centred more on motions of condemnation of the 'junta's' reactionary legislation and policies.

Recently released Northern Ireland cabinet files from the 1920s reveal early contacts between the Free State government and the Northern administration of Sir James Craig. Mr Cosgrave wrote to Sir James as early as 1923 concerning the welfare of Irish prisoners jailed in the North for political offences committed there in 1922.

One of the areas in which the Free State government made extraordinary advances was that of the development of external relations policy. Mr Cosgrave brought Ireland into the League of Nations in 1923, a move which the British did not welcome. Ireland was elected to the Council of the League of Nations in September 1930, thus achieving a voice in an important international forum. De Valera made very effective use of that voice within a couple of years of the accession of Ireland to the Council.

The Free State government also played no small part in securing the passing of the Statute of Westminster in December 1931 which improved considerably the lot of dominion parliaments. Mr Cosgrave played an extremely clever game in order to secure the passing of the statute, outwitting even its most vocal opponent, Winston Churchill. However, at home no political capital could be made from such successes.

Behind the scenes W.T. Cosgrave had also made attempts to persuade the British to abolish the oath of allegiance. Some historians see his motivation as primarily his own political survival, coupled with his desire to be seen to stick firmly to the letter of the Treaty. His message to London was, essentially, remove the oath or de Valera will use it as a weapon to win the election.

As the campaign got underway the ambiguity which surrounded Lemass's relationship with the IRA surfaced again. He liaised with at least one, and possibly more, IRA officers in Dublin. Together they studied electoral lists to ensure that republican sympathisers voted for Fianna Fáil. Recent attempts at personation pale into insignificance beside the efforts of the IRA support groups to secure the votes, not just of the living, but of the dead and the sons and daughters of Erin who had emigrated.

Otherwise Lemass was busy structuring the economic elements of the party's election manifesto. The party strategists concentrated on the stick with which they would beat the Cosgrave government: failure to develop Irish industry, over-expenditure, partition, and most significantly, the land annuities payable to Britain.

Irish tenant farmers payed half-yearly annuities to the Land Commission which passed them on to London. They were payable in return for a loan from Britain which turned Irish tenant farmers into proprietors. Fianna Fáil promised to rid the country of the annuities. The party argued that since the land in question was sovereign Irish territory the British had no right to claim the £3,000,000 annual payment. What was not mentioned in the election propaganda was that Fianna Fáil in government intended the money to be paid into the Irish Treasury.

The eventual withholding of the annuities led to the economic war with Britain and caused major headaches for Lemass's ministry.

The package put forward by Fianna Fáil did little to assuage the fears of the party's usual detractors. In Dublin Lemass instructed his canvassers to stress on the doorsteps that Fianna Fáil was not in favour of communism. At a time when the 'red scare' was very much in evidence this move was meant to placate a reluctant Roman Catholic hierarchy. Some months before the election the hierarchy issued a pastoral warning of the evils of communism and illegal activities.

Fianna Fáil's manifesto also promised to end partition but not before consulting the people.

Balanced against a cautious law and order package from Cumann na nGaedheal, the Fianna Fáil election package had a broader appeal and on 16 February 1932 the people voted for change.

That change did not have an easy birth.

The election campaign was very far from a gentlemanly affair. Election meetings of both Fianna Fáil and Cumann na nGaedheal were broken up by violent clashes. Candidates appeared at the hustings carrying revolvers; Civil War slogans were hurled as terms of political abuse; Fianna Fáil used IRA volunteers as bodyguards while Cumann na nGaedheal used the police in similar fashion; all sides claimed widespread personation and ballot rigging. Out of that mayhem was born the first Fianna Fáil administration.

Fianna Fáil won 43.7 per cent of the first preference votes and 72 seats; Cumann na nGaedheal won 35.3 per cent and 57 seats; Labour 7.7 per cent and 7 seats; Farmers 3.1 per cent and 4 seats; Independents 7.8 per cent and 11 seats and two outgoing Labour TDs were returned as Independent Labour.

With the support of Labour and three Independents, Fianna Fáil formed a government. On Tuesday 9 March 1932 de Valera and his deputies – several of them carrying revolvers – entered Leinster House to assume the reins of government.

Fears of a coup were uppermost in the minds of Fianna Fáil deputies as they passed through the crowds who had gathered all morning in Kildare Street. However, Lemass was one of the deputies who did not carry a gun to that historic meeting of Dáil

Éireann. In the morning he attended a votive mass for the work of the new Dáil in the Pro-Cathedral. In the afternoon he made his way to Leinster House.

'Intense Excitement Marks Change Of Government' the *Irish Press* proclaimed in its headline. 'Fianna Fáil's First Government Chosen' the *Irish Independent* announced more soberly on the same day, 10 March.

The public gallery was crowded. Again Mrs Pearse was present to see the historic event. The distinguished visitors' gallery contained diplomatic representatives of the United States, France, Italy, Belgium, Poland and other states.

Lemass entered the chamber alone, exchanged a smile with P.J. Ruttledge and took his seat. Frank Fahy was elected Ceann Comhairle [Speaker] of the Dáil and de Valera was elected President of the Executive by 81 votes to 68. Amongst the Independents who supported him was James Dillon, a future leader of Fine Gael.

The Governor-General took the unusual step of arriving at Leinster House, rather than receiving the new appointee at his official residence, the Vice-Regal Lodge. He had to return again in the evening when Lemass and the other ministers received their appointments from him.

The newspapers of the following day announced the new cabinet.

Eamon de Valera was President of the Executive and Minister for External Affairs; Sean T. O'Kelly, Vice-President and Minister for Local Government; Seán MacEntee, Minister for Finance; Seán Lemass, Minister for Industry and Commerce; James Geoghegan, Minister for Justice; James Ryan, Minister for Agriculture; Frank Aiken, Minister for Defence; P.J. Ruttledge, Minister for Lands and Fisheries; Tom Derrig, Minister for Education and Joseph Connolly, Minister for Posts & Telegraphs. Joseph Connolly was the only member of the cabinet not a member of the Dáil, he was a member of the Senate and the first member of the Upper House to be given a ministerial post.

The *Irish Press* also reported that day the intention of the new government to suspend the notorious 'Safety Act' and to abolish the oath. The paper also reported a dramatic visit to Arbour Hill Prison by the new Ministers for Justice and Defence where they inspected the conditions under which political prisoners were being held and ordered an immediate improvement.

The *Irish Independent* carried profiles of the new ministers. It gave a short outline of Lemass's military activities, gave the wrong year of his first election to the Dáil and mentioned that he was one of the joint honorary secretaries of Fianna Fáil.

The following day, Friday 11 March, Lemass went to his department to meet his staff and to begin his ministerial career. He was 32 years old and the youngest member of the cabinet.

6

THE BENJAMIN OF THE CABINET

When Seán Lemass took over the helm at the Department of Industry and Commerce he found it, in his own words, a government department 'rotting through inaction'. He confided to his wife that he would have preferred the Finance portfolio. She alone knew of his disappointment until many years later when he discussed with de Valera how his appointment to Finance might have altered the course of government policy in that area.

His predecessor in the Cumann na nGaedheal administration, Patrick McGilligan, had held simultaneously the posts of Minister for External Affairs and the Industry and Commerce portfolio. The Dáil debates for the period make it quite clear which brief McGilligan held to be of greater significance. The record also shows that Lemass, as opposition spokesman, was highly critical not just of department policy but of the way in which McGilligan handled Industry and Commerce and its affairs.

Lemass's disappointment in not receiving Finance did not affect his attitude to his appointment at Industry and Commerce, nor did the appointment diminish in any way his place in the pecking order within the new cabinet.

That was made quite clear when, in May 1932, a cabinet committee was established to 'examine and report to the cabinet on the economic conditions of the Saorstát'. The committee consisted of de Valera, Lemass, the Minister for Agriculture, James Ryan, and the Minister for Posts & Telegraphs, Joseph Connolly. Curiously the Minister for Finance, Seán MacEntee, was omitted from the committee and also from the delegation which attended the Imperial Economic Conference in Ottawa later that summer. That forum was Lemass's first major appearance representing Ireland on the world political stage and though the conference itself was something of a damp squib in terms of the ineffectiveness of its conclusions, Lemass is reported to have handled his brief extremely well for someone who had just settled in to his new ministry.

The day after the Governor-General appointed the cabinet, de Valera moved to allay fears within the civil service that a new broom would be sweeping clean throughout its ranks. In keeping with that spirit Lemass went to his department to meet his staff. He gave instructions that those who wished to cooperate with his policies were welcome to stay and those who did not were welcome to move on. The new minister chose as his head of department, John Leydon, who had earned a reputation as one of the more dynamic of the new breed of civil servant. The historian Dr Ronan Fanning has described the partnership as one which 'proved among the most formidable of its kind in the history of the state'. Brian Farrell observes that it was an unlikely alliance:

> Leydon was a career civil servant whose abilities quickly attracted attention from the mandarins of the new Irish service. He became a Finance man. Involved in both the all-party Economic Committee and the Tariff Commission...Leydon took the trouble to indicate that he did not agree with the policies and ideas expressed in Lemass's speeches. Lemass replied brusquely that he was not looking for a 'yes-man' and would be prepared to accept reasonable argued advice.

Immediately upon taking over command of his department Lemass let it be known that as minister he would be leading from the front. In 1969 he told Michael Mills that he had gathered around him a group of officials who could be relied upon to 'do very competently anything that had to be done'. This attitude presupposed that he could get cabinet approval for the type of reforms he wished to implement. However, he was to find that such approval was not always forthcoming, indeed some of his early proposals met with considerable cabinet resistance. It was a cautious cabinet and civil service which Lemass faced in 1932 when it came to matters of economic policy development.

De Valera was anxious to show the public that he and his ministers cared enough about the economic situation they had inherited to reduce his own and his ministers' salaries substantially. The move can hardly have been welcomed by an already financially hard-pressed Seán Lemass. He found it necessary to supplement his salary by applying for a pension based on his record of service during 1916 and the War of Independence. He applied for and was granted that pension.

The economic condition of the country as a whole in 1932 is reflected in a memorandum prepared for the cabinet by the Department of Finance and quoted by Ronan Fanning in his superb history of that department. The memorandum says the situation was:

> ...undoubtedly gloomy. Nor can the immediate outlook be said to hold any definite promise of relief. There are at present no grounds for holding the view that world economic conditions will improve in the immediate future, while, on the other hand, there is considerable danger that conditions may become definitely worse than they are now. The position, therefore, is that the national income of the Saorstát has fallen seriously in recent years while, on the other hand, the real burden of taxation has been seriously increased. The situation cannot be remedied merely by increasing taxation; and it must not be overlooked that an attempt to find £3 million by new taxation would seriously interfere with the consumption of many commodities which are at present a source of very substantial revenue.

The memorandum was written at a time when de Valera was considering how best to implement his economic nationalism so that he might create his self-sufficient rural society. It came at a time when Lemass was adding to his plans for Ireland's industrialisation: protection for industry and price support for agriculture.

Lemass, and all other members of the cabinet, were aware how their policy decisions were constrained by the pledges made to the Labour Party in return for its support in the voting lobby.

One of the pledges posed no particular problem for Lemass's plans as it involved a firm promise to implement industrial protection. Also promised was an effective strategy on unemployment and that the country's resources would be developed in an effective manner.

Lemass set about implementing his policy of protection which he had lauded as a necessary expedient soon after entering Dáil Éireann. The first protective tariffs had been imposed by Cumann na nGaedheal in the budget of 1924 to give what Lemass's predecessor, McGilligan called 'a limited experiment in the use of a tariff for the stimulation of Irish industry'.

Lemass must have found considerable comfort in a lecture delivered by the economist John Maynard Keynes in Dublin in April 1933. Keynes had a considerable influence on the development of Lemass's economic thinking and his endorsement of the government's policy of self-sufficiency can only have pleased the young minister:

> I sympathize with those who would minimize rather than those who would maximise, economic entanglement between nations. Ideas, knowledge, science, hospitality, travel – these are the things which should of their nature be international. But let goods be homespun whenever it is reasonable and conveniently possible, and, above all, let finance be primarily national....If I were an Irishman I should find much to attract me in the economic outlook of your present government towards self-sufficiency.

While the benediction of the eminent economist was reassuring, even the most ardent supporters of Keynes in Ireland were aware that there were particular structural difficulties which faced Irish industry. By 1939 Lemass was certainly aware of the limitations which Keynes himself had identified. The small size of the home market made it difficult for new Irish industries to expand. On the international front competition was keen, particularly because manufacturing costs were so high in Ireland.

While Lemass was ruthless in his application of his protectionist policy, he did admit that there was not always a clear picture of its merits. But in 1928 he had spoken passionately of the need for such a policy:

> Ireland can be made a self-contained unit, providing all the necessities of living are in adequate quantities for the people residing in the island at the moment and probably for a much larger number.... Until we get a definite national policy decided on in favour of industrial and agricultural protection and an executive in office prepared to enforce that policy, it is useless to hope for results.

The depression of the 1930s marked a world-wide abandonment of free-trade policies and a movement towards stringent protectionism. The government's policy of self-sufficiency was aimed at domestic production replacing imports as far as possible. Under Lemass's policy of protection customs duties were raised and applied to a wide variety of products.

Lemass also advocated extending direct controls, including the imposition of quotas. He was adamant that in the industrial sphere protection would be extended beyond the bounds of just existing industries and would be used to promote the establishment of new industries as well.

In addition he advised that protectionist policies be employed to ensure the decentralisation of native industry by granting the umbrella of protection only to those industries if they established in areas which the government was promoting. Decentralisation fitted in neatly with de Valera's bucolic dream, as it ensured that factories were established in rural areas where agricultural employment was not sufficient to keep the population from emigrating to the cities or abroad.

Lemass introduced the Customs Duties (Provisional Imposition) Act and used three Finance Acts of 1932 to impose duties on a wide range of goods. The Emergency Imposition of Duties Act was used to penalise British imports after the outbreak of the economic war over the land annuities row.

The effects of that economic war on Fianna Fáil's chances of retaining power might have been detrimental had de Valera, with Lemass's help, not moved to prevent such a disaster by introducing a package of measures aimed specifically at avoiding it.

The millions of the retained land annuities were spent at home to cushion the blow of the loss of Britain as Ireland's biggest export market. Before the economic war Britain accounted for 96 per cent of the Free State's export market. The majority of that was made up of agricultural exports.

The Department of Finance's prediction for the 1932 budget shortfall was put at around £3,000,000. The civil service was horrified at the prospect of the effects of the economic war on external trade and its long-term effects on the economy. Ministers were expected to find alternative markets and it fell to Lemass to diversify Irish industry to cope with the loss of the British market.

De Valera was determined that the Irish people should be prepared to wade in behind him and that no effort should be spared to maintain national dignity in the face of what he saw as this latest attack from the old enemy. His government, he told the Dáil on 5 August, was not expecting to 'have omelettes without cracking eggs'.

By December 1932 the trade figures showed that the volume of exports had dropped by half. Efforts to secure new markets in Europe and to increase the export drive to the United States did not come near compensating for the loss of the British market. Lemass's despair at the situation is evident from a memorandum he wrote in November in which he likened the potential situation that might be created to that of the famine of 1847:

I do not think it can be denied that we are facing a crisis as grave as that of 1847 and I feel strongly that our present efforts are totally inadequate to deal with it...a collapse of our economic position is in sight.

Early efforts to resolve the annuities dispute failed. Britain was convinced that it would be the undoing of de Valera and as if to prove that opinion British officials maintained contact with leading figures in Cumann na nGaedheal on the understanding that Mr de Valera would soon be vacating his office. Seán MacEntee may have had these contacts in mind when he spoke in the Dáil of the 'knaves and traitors who spread the spirit of faction amongst us'.

In a further memorandum Lemass said he saw little hope of an immediate improvement in the trade deficit and he proposed what Ronan Fanning has called 'a board whose existence would have had far-reaching consequences for the Department of Finance'. It could have moved the balance of power on economic matters in the direction of Lemass's own department. He proposed the establishment of the Board for External Trade which would act in all matters of policy subject to the Minister for Industry and Commerce who would consult with the Minister for Agriculture where agricultural interests were involved. Again the memorandum states bluntly Lemass's fears about the consequences of the economic war:

> The situation is black. It is, to say the least, doubtful if we are in a position to maintain the 'economic war'. It is equally doubtful if the termination of the 'economic war' will alone greatly improve out situation. We have reached the point where a collapse of our economic system is in sight. By a collapse, I mean famine conditions for a large number of our people.

Drastic situations often require drastic remedies and Lemass proposed just such a set of remedies. They included the reduction of agricultural production to the minimum for home supply and export requirements; taking off the land all persons not needed to achieve that requirement; employment on public works schemes for the unemployed; reduction of imports to essentials.

He was aware as he framed the proposals that they would need, as he put it, 'dictatorial powers for their execution'. The

Department of Finance resisted the proposals. Apart from professional objections the officials knew that it was unlikely that such measures would have had a smooth passage through the Dáil or at the cabinet table.

Lemass became increasingly aware of this as the brief honeymoon period of cabinet cosiness translated into the more usual forms of cabinet wrangling. Lemass did not meet opposition on all of the proposals but the principle opponents were Seán MacEntee and Joseph Connolly. On most policy matters there was usually accord amongst ministers. Indeed the Fianna Fáil cabinets of the 1930s were remarkable for the absence of dissension amongst ministers.

Lemass and his fellow ministers were conscious of the fact the whatever proposals they raised at cabinet would have to fit in not just with Fianna Fáil policy but they would also have to pay at least lip-service to de Valera's vision of Ireland.

The economic war allowed Lemass considerable scope in the introduction of protection, as it was used to harness the patriotic mood in the country to encourage greater self-sufficiency. The government could therefore present the move towards economic independence as something that ran in tandem with political independence. The reality however was that the fall-out from the land annuities dispute caused serious problems for small farmers as well as for the 'ranchers' who were Cumann na nGaedheal supporters. The policy of protection failed to produce the desired level of self-sufficiency. Lemass's protectionist policies brought about a situation of near monopoly in some industries thus causing excessive price rises. This led to the Control of Prices Act which provided for the establishment of the Prices Commission which sought to control the price of protected products and keep them from being unduly high.

The view has often been put forward that de Valera left economic policy matters very much in the hands of Lemass, as he himself forged ahead with his bucolic vision and with constitutional issues. More recent scholarship has given credit to the partnership which existed between de Valera and Lemass on economic matters. It was the very fact that this 'partnership' existed which allowed Lemass to construct his Keynesian blueprint for Irish economic development.

That Lemass actively canvassed de Valera's support for that blueprint is evident from the large number of private memoranda in which Lemass sought to win over the 'Chief' before taking his plans to cabinet. The process occasionally worked in reverse. Lemass would contact de Valera after he had met with resistance within the cabinet.

Thus we find him writing a personal letter to de Valera on 14 November 1932 on the unemployment question. Unsure that it was his direct area of responsibility, he wrote:

> I have two definite proposals to put which, if adopted, will cope adequately with the situation, in my opinion. I am putting them in this personal way rather than through my department because I am not clear that the initiation of proposals of this character is my official responsibility and from the nature of the proposals you will see that other departments are directly involved. I think, therefore, that it is preferable that you should bring them up for consideration by the council, [cabinet] if you can.

The two proposals were of a practical nature. The first proposed legislation to protect the unemployed from eviction for non-payment of rent; the second proposed to establish weekly unemployment assistance subject to a means test. The weekly payment would apply to all unemployed over 18 years of age. Lemass calculated that on the basis of the existing unemployment figures the scheme would cost £1,500,000 a year. He proposed to raise the money to fund the scheme from an increase in urban and county council rates with the shortfall of £325,000 being made up by a state contribution. The Unemployment Assistance Act 1933 extended considerably the classes of person eligible for unemployment assistance.

Brian Farrell observes that Lemass's letter to de Valera reveals some enduring characteristics of his political aims, style and methods '...the impatience to short-circuit discussion and procedure, the demand for decision and action, the recognition, to adapt Truman's phrase, that the buck starts with the head of government'.

Despite his attempts to appeal to de Valera, Lemass's proposals met with resistance from the Department of Finance and his attempt to protect the unemployed from eviction was rejected by his colleagues on the economic committee. So too was his plan for national reorganisation. The cabinet fudged on the matter, rejecting some of the proposals out of hand and deferring others.

It was now December 1932.

At that time the alliance between Fianna Fáil and Labour was coming under considerable strain. Various factors contributed to this situation. Labour was making what Fianna Fáil saw as excessive demands for legislation; demands often based on knowledge gained at the weekly briefings between Labour deputies and government ministers.

Lemass was particularly unhappy with the way in which Labour, in his view, used the information gleaned at those meetings to make its own political capital. He was pleased therefore to see the alliance crumble over a proposed cut in civil service pay.

The decision to call an election for February 1933 rested, of course, with de Valera, however accounts differ as to whether he did or did not consult his ministers. Lemass recalled that de Valera did seek his advice and he counselled his leader to dissolve the Dáil and have another election before Labour had an opportunity to vote against the proposed pay cuts. Whatever or whomsoever prompted it, this is exactly what de Valera decided upon.

It appears the election came as a surprise to most of de Valera's ministers but it is certain that the announcement, at a midnight press conference, came as a considerable surprise to all in Cumann na nGaedheal.

The campaign got underway with a promise from Fianna Fáil to cut farmer's annuity payments by half and to be an administration which cared for the poor. For the most part the party's manifesto differed little from that of the 1932 election. The party promised that if returned to power it would consolidate reforms already set in train. It would continue to dismantle the state created by the Treaty but no major constitutional changes were promised. The emergence of the Centre Party worried both Fianna Fáil and Cumann na nGaedheal but the latter feared that the middle-of-the-road policies of the new party would attract those who were disillusioned with its policies and who would never consider voting for Fianna Fáil. The party was also still reeling from the shock of its defeat and was not well prepared to fight the election.

The IRA decided to uphold its policy of working against Cosgrave and not openly endorsing Fianna Fáil, yet as usual, republicans did work for Fianna Fáil. And in scenes that presaged greater troubles to come, the election saw several violent clashes between republican supporters and the Army Comrades Association which some of its members saw as an auxiliary force to the police.

Lemass was again appointed director of elections. Fianna Fáil won 49.7 per cent of the first preference vote and 77 seats; Cumann na nGaedheal 30.5 per cent and 48 seats; Labour 5.7 per cent and 8 seats; Centre Party 9.1 per cent and 11 seats; and Independents 5 per cent and 9 seats. Fianna Fáil was returned to power with a majority of one and increased it by another seat gained at a by-election in 1934.

Lemass increased his personal vote by 4,000 and was returned at the head of the poll. He survived cabinet changes in the new administration to hold on to his ministry, thus enabling him to continue the task he had begun.

At 33 he was still the youngest member of the government, or as de Valera was fond of calling him 'the Benjamin of the cabinet'.

7

'MY MOST ABLE MINISTER'

With the 1933 election behind him Lemass began to apply himself to the process of putting his own ineradicable stamp on the government's economic policy. Fianna Fáil, in its early years in power pursued an economic policy line which was a curious mix of radical agrarianism coupled with a push towards industrialisation. It was meant to have a broad appeal and in those early years it had just such an appeal. The party was able to rely on the votes of middle-sized and small farmers, shopkeepers and lower middle-class urban voters and in limited measure on the urban working-class. It came to power with a programme which promised radical reform. Its image in 1933 was very much that of a progressive party.

The strongly nationalist nature of Lemass's own views did not colour his tough attitude towards the more sentimental and traditional of Fianna Fáil's policies such as its call to have as many families as was practicable upon the land. By the end of the 1930s even de Valera was aware that his bucolic vision was, in real terms, a non-starter. Despite an aggressive pro-agrarian policy, which included large scale land redistribution, the flight from the land continued to be a painful reality for de Valera. By the end of the decade he admitted this openly saying that 'there is no use hoping that we can put back the clock'.

Ironically, the failure of that vision contributed much to the making of Seán Lemass's role as the avatar of economic change. That role, however, contributed to the often expressed view of him that he lacked any understanding of rural Ireland. It was a view which found expression not just with the opposition but also within Fianna Fáil. His old sparring partner Senator Joseph Connolly, Minister for Lands, reinforced this view of Lemass when he accused him of neglecting Gaeltacht industries. In February 1935 Connolly offered this opinion to the cabinet:

> There is growing impatience with the government's so-called neglect of the Gaeltacht areas with regard to industrial development. This has been expressed at party meetings by deputies representing Gaeltacht con-stituencies....The policy for industrial development is entirely one for the Minister for Industry and Commerce and in directing and influencing manufacturing concerns the Minister, will, no doubt, experience difficulty in inducing them to ignore the eastern seaboard....Nevertheless, we have, I feel, reached the position when we must decide whether we mean to do anything to provide employment in the Gaeltacht areas or if our policy is one of acceptance of the idea that it is neither practical nor advisable to direct or divert certain industries to those areas.

Lemass weathered the storm with Connolly over the Gaeltacht areas but many country deputies continued to hold the view that he had an urban bias even when he was Taoiseach. The late Paddy Lindsay, Fine Gael deputy, senator and Master of the High Court, also held such a view of Lemass:

> He was direct, unpretentious and open. His energy and his enthusiasm were very evident. My only complaint would be that he had little or no understanding of rural Ireland. He was the essential city man.

Between 1933 and 1948 Lemass laid the foundations of an economic policy which he would continue to develop as minister, Tánaiste and Taoiseach. There were four general elections during those years, after all of which Fianna Fáil formed a government. The first was in July 1937 and it saw Fianna Fáil once more dependant on Labour support. In May 1938 Labour withdrew that support thus precipitating a general election in June which gave Fianna Fáil 77 seats and allowed it form a majority government which lasted the full term of five years. By that time the economic war had ended but the benefits which had accrued were short-lived. By the general election of June 1943 the hardships brought about by the Second World War or 'Emergency' as it was known in Ireland, lost Fianna Fáil ten seats and its overall majority in the Dáil. However, with the support of some independents it formed a minority government. In May 1944 that administration was defeated on a Transport Bill, and de Valera, strengthened by his role as national leader during the 'Emergency', called a general election which returned Fianna Fáil to power as a majority government. They remained in power until 1948. In the elections of 1943 and 1944 Lemass polled the highest number of votes cast for any candidate – over 15,000 – thus strengthening his hand and allowing him considerable prestige within his own party. Let us now look at how he used that position to further his economic policies.

As we have already seen the course of Lemass's plans did not always run smooth and he continued to encounter resistance within the cabinet, principally from the same two sources, Seán MacEntee and Senator Joseph Connolly (until Fianna Fáil abolished the Senate) but also from Frank Aiken whom he was sharply critical of on a number of issues, including a proposal Aiken had for a new volunteer force in the army. Liam Skinner in his near hagiographical essay in *Politicians By Accident* hints at this resistance when he refers to the 'unusual opposition and obstacles' which Lemass encountered as he went about laying the 'foundations of Ireland's industrial arm'. In the creation and development of a whole raft of state-promoted companies, ranging from the Industrial Credit Company to Bord na Móna and Irish Life Assurance Lemass learned with consummate ease how best to deal with objections from his colleagues at the cabinet table.

Some projects were greeted with more enthusiasm than others. In 1936 Lemass began to put shape to his plans for a national airline. Flying in Ireland began with the Army Air Corps, formed in 1922 after the British departed. Ireland had been established on the aviation map since Alcock and Brown landed in a field in Connemara in 1919. Lemass authorised the establishment of Aer Lingus with capital of £100,000 and while progress was slow initially it did become a success story until more recent times.

The fact that Lemass was the youngest member of cabinet did not prevent him from being critical of his older colleagues. He was often impatient with their reticent approach to his ideas and that led him to be assertive not just in the tone of his verbal criticism but also in memoranda and in letters. One such letter to MacEntee indicates that their differences were founded on arguments other than the purely ideological. Lemass wrote to his colleague on 5 May 1938 to dress him down for concentrating Fianna Fáil speakers, especially ministers, in the Dublin Townships constituency (MacEntee's own). He reminded him that Fianna Fáil was fighting the election in 34 other constituencies. MacEntee replied a month later defending his position.

Lemass was fortunate that de Valera favoured a policy of judicious delegation which allowed his ministers a considerable degree of autonomy, especially in the more unpopular decisions which de Valera wished to distance himself from. De Valera's biographers, Longford and O'Neill, observed the relationship between the Taoiseach and his minister thus:

> He gave his able Minister for Industry and Commerce confidence and support, in full measure, which were invaluable throughout the years, particularly whenever doubts and reservations occurred on the part of other members of the government. Yet the outlook of the two men on economic and social matters was not identical.

This degree of autonomy suited Lemass's purposes. By 1940, however, when war had isolated Ireland and the emigration routes remained open as a safety valve against any possible threat to social stability posed by the army of unemployed, Lemass had long since realised that de Valera's dream of a closed society was becoming something of a nightmare for him as Minister for Industry and Commerce.

Within its first year in office Fianna Fáil's economic and social policy had already taken on a settled appearance and most members of the cabinet were happy to endorse it now.

Lemass continued to try and create a class of native industrialist who would help him diversify the structure of the Irish economy. Though Lemass's protectionist policies did help to strike a better balance between industry and agriculture, he admitted after the war that those policies came at a high cost. But in 1937 he offered this stout defence of his policies when he spoke at a factory opening in Athy on 10 May:

> Industrial progress had been so rapid in the last few years that mistakes were nearly inevitable, but I do not admit they were either numerous or serious. During that time, I acted on the principle that the only way to avert mistakes was to do nothing. As I did not intend to do nothing, I discounted the mistakes in advance.

In the same year de Valera was wrestling with the introduction of a new constitution. Lemass has rarely been credited with instituting changes in social policy or with taking an interest in constitutional matters. Yet it was he who said to de Valera when the 1937 Constitution was being drafted: 'You know, Chief, we can't very well make the Constitution a manifesto of Fianna Fáil social policy.' Lemass believed that progress in the area of social services would follow as a result of the successful implementation of his economic policy. The Dáil debates for the 1930s show the wide range of social issues he addressed, particularly matters relating to housing, pensions and unemployment benefit.

In the period under discussion many social welfare benefits were introduced, most notably widow's and orphan's pensions and recognition of the state's obligations to the unemployed. In the first decade of the Fianna Fáil administration over 130,000 houses were built or reconstructed. Some progress was also made in the area of the health services. Little real progress could be achieved, however, as long as the economic war with Britain still raged. De Valera's vision was bolstered by certain aspects of the economic war and Lemass went along with endorsing de Valera's economic fiction. He made no public admission of this fact, rather he argued that the measures imposed on the country at the time of the economic war were not a consequence of it, but were designed to 'provide more effective machinery to develop the industrial activities and the industrial potentialities' of the country.

The general election of 1937 left Fianna Fáil with a reduced power-base and it was again dependant on the support of Labour. The acceptance by the electorate of the new constitution was not enough to reassure a government which faced, as its most pressing problem, the devastating effects of the economic war.

As the Second World War approached Lemass was one of the key strategists involved in the negotiations to end the economic war. Various attempts, secret and open, to de-escalate the conflict were made, including the coal-cattle pact of 1934 and the cement-cattle pact of 1936. However, no real progress was made until the Irish and British negotiating teams sat down to discuss their differences in London.

The cabinet approved the Irish team in January 1938. It was made up of de Valera, Lemass, Seán MacEntee and Jim Ryan. All three had actively pressed within cabinet for an early conclusion to the economic war. Frank Aiken, who had responsibility for defence, was not included in the Irish side. It fell to Lemass to secure the best possible deal for Ireland on the economic front. He was motivated by his personal desire to be rid of what he saw as the subversive effect the conflict was having on his efforts at the Department of Industry and Commerce. He found his hand considerably strengthened by the fact that the British were anxious to settle the economic war. De Valera, who was more concerned with gaining ground on the partition question, left London without securing the advance he had hoped for. He did, however, secure the return of the Irish ports held by Britain. The British had retained Berehaven, Cobh, Belfast Lough, and Lough Swilly and oil depot facilities at Haulbowline and Rathmullan.

Lemass correctly felt that Ireland was in a stronger position in regard to the trade negotiations than on the separate issues of partition and defence. Thus he successfully secured free entry (with limited exceptions) into the British market for Irish industrial goods. Protective tariffs could be maintained and there was to be equal market access for Irish and British farmers. For a minister anxious to progress Irish economic growth, such a successful conclusion to the economic war was a boon.

The signing of the Anglo-Irish Agreement on 25 April 1938 was a major landmark in Lemass's ministerial career for it allowed him the scope to proceed with his economic vision. In the course of the next 28 years he would receive many invitations to dine with heads of state and of government. After his death one of the few such invitations found amongst his papers was Chamberlain's invitation to lunch at 10 Downing Street to mark the signing of that historic agreement.

On the 28 April Lemass outlined to the Dáil the provisions of the Trade Agreement which it was asked to approve. He explained to the House the difference between the ports agreement and the agreements which affected finance and trade and he outlined the bearing the trade agreement would have on the government's economic policy. During the course of his remarks he referred to the relationship between the United Kingdom and Ireland as 'one which is not parallelled between any other two countries on earth'. He told the House it was not possible to negotiate a trade agreement upon the 'winner take all' basis.

> There is a fundamental difference between negotiating an agreement and the process of backing a horse. A trade agreement is essentially a bargain similar to the bargain that takes place when a farmer brings a cow to a fair. In this case the British government was selling the cow, the cow being free entry to the British market. Just as a farmer will not sell his cow unless he thinks the price offered for it is equal to its value so also, the dealer will not buy the cow if he thinks the price is in excess of the value, or more than he can afford to pay. The dealer naturally will dislike every penny by which his first offer has to be increased in order to get the transaction

completed. Similarly, many of the provisions of this Agreement were accepted by the negotiators with reluctance. I am sure it is true to say the same of the British negotiators, that many of the provisions of the Agreement were accepted by them with reluctance. When we went over to London to negotiate a trade agreement we had two primary aims in view...to secure free entry for our products into the British market...and to preserve our powers to promote and assist industrial development here.

In 1938 two other issues, apart from the general election, dominated Lemass's agenda. On the first of these, the report of the commission on banking, he again found himself in conflict with Seán MacEntee. The establishment of the Free State brought no immediate change to the monetary system. British currency and cheques drawn on British banks were accepted in Ireland and cheques drawn on Irish banks were accepted in Britain. A Banking Commission was established in 1926 but it made no changes to the status quo. Another commission was appointed in 1934 and it reported in March 1938 with minority reports in August. Its terms of reference were 'to examine and report on the system in Saorstát Éireann of currency, banking, credit, public borrowing and lending, and the pledging of state credit on behalf of agriculture, industry and the social services, and to consider and report what changes, if any, are necessary or desirable to promote the social and economic welfare of the community and the interests of agriculture and industry'.

The commission found in favour of the status quo, recommending the retention of parity with sterling, tight control on semi-state borrowing and the establishment of a currency commission to act as a central bank. The report was critical of de Valera's self-sufficiency programme. In real terms little progress had been made since the establishment of the 1926 commission. Lemass, who opposed the establishment of the commission found this situation wholly unsatisfactory. De Valera appeared to show little interest in the majority report and apart from driving a further wedge between Lemass and MacEntee the somewhat conservative commission can be said to have achieved little, though indirectly it led to the passing of the Central Bank Act in 1942.

Lemass favoured the establishment of a banking authority with real financial teeth. Again he encountered resistance from Finance, and its new minister Seán T. O'Kelly. Finance used the arguments of the Banking Commission to oppose the type of Central Bank which Lemass wished to see established. Lemass wrote:

> The Government has decided that a Central Bank is be established. It is desired that the Central Bank should possess power to influence the credit position within the country...[and] have power which can be used, in circumstances in which the Board of the Bank deem it desirable so to do, to make it more profitable for the commercial banks to increase their loans to internal borrowers, or in other circumstances to decrease such loans. The Central Bank may rarely, ever, have occasion to use such power but its possession will place it in a position to influence the credit policy of the commercial banks.... It is no argument against it that no other central bank has compulsory powers of the same nature. No other country has precisely the same circumstances, and in any case, there is no standard pattern of central bank.

Banking was not the only area in which Lemass met with civil service and cabinet resistance in his early years at Industry and Commerce. His efforts to develop Ireland's capacity to refine oil were also stonewalled. A plan to grant a monopoly to an Irish-based refining company was drawn up by Industry and Commerce when Cumann na nGaedheal were still in power. The plan was rejected but Lemass revived and developed it in 1935. The Department of Finance raised a number of objections, most especially that of viability. MacEntee wrote directly to de Valera, essentially saying that he was washing his hands of the project on the basis that the Lemass proposals were 'not equitable to our people' and were 'too greedy'. The opposition voiced certain reservations in the Dáil. It tabled questions to the minister concerning the conditions of employment of those already employed in Irish oil distribution and what compensation would be offered those displaced by the proposed monopoly. Lemass was also questioned on the possible pollution threat to bathing places in Dublin. Lemass replied that it was not his intention to displace existing oil distribution workers and said his information was that no waste would be thrown into Dublin Harbour. There were further and more difficult hurdles to be encountered as Lemass stubbornly pressed ahead.

It seemed that no proposal of Lemass's would be complete without the objections of Senator Connolly, the Minister for Lands, and true to form the minister circulated a memorandum which stated bluntly that 'the whole plan and scheme is unsatisfactory from the point of view of national economic interest'. Even the Attorney General joined in the chorus of disapproval, saying that while he had no desire to hamper the Minister for Industry and Commerce he found that 'loosely worded agreements...are the source of endless trouble'. The AG was correct in the latter assumption; the project did cause endless trouble. Lemass secured cabinet approval and entered into an agreement with the Thames Oil Water Company and work began on the construction of a refinery at Dublin's North Wall.

While Lemass successfully flexed his muscles at the cabinet table in Dublin his writ did not extend to the City of London where the might of the Shell Oil Company was ranged against him. Back-room wrangling succeeded in Shell forcing Thames Oil Water out of the project but undaunted, Lemass secured the support of the shipping magnate Andrew Weir who undertook to partner Lemass's scheme. At that juncture however a force greater than the London financial moguls intervened to thwart the scheme. The world was in the grip of war and Lemass channelled his energies into his new portfolio as Minister for Supplies. Brian Farrell writes of him at this period:

If the first seven years in Industry and Commerce had proved him an energetic, skilful and innovative ministerial tradesman, the next phase of his career showed his capacity to practice his craft in a different and larger context.

The period which lay ahead was not a fertile time for the development of Irish economic policy, and Lemass had to channel, what were now the skills of a very formidable cabinet minister, in a new direction.

8

HALF-OUNCE LEMASS

Sheila Lemass recalls her father receiving what might appear a somewhat unusual gift if it were not for the fact that the Second World War was raging at the time. A diplomat presented him with a chest of tea – a highly prized commodity in the days of rampant war shortages and rationing. The family was overjoyed at the prospect – Mrs Lemass particularly, as it was her favourite tipple. To the amazement and intense annoyance of his family he returned the gift to the ambassador, explaining to his children that if the Irish people had to suffer deprivation, so too would the Lemass family. During the war friends also pressed gifts on him, which were always refused. Peggy Lemass remembers Gerry O'Sullivan, a Dublin merchant, also sending a gift of tea which her father returned. She also remembers an international jewellery manufacturer who was anxious to set up in Ireland, receiving the same reaction to his gifts when they were pressed on the family. These were but a few small examples, *in vacuo*, of how the mind of the man, who had been appointed Minister for Supplies by de Valera, was working at that time.

At the outbreak of war Lemass was concerned for the safety of his children and he arranged for them to be sent to Ballina, in the belief that it was less likely to be bombed than Dublin. His wife objected and the children saw out most of the war in Skerries, where Maureen Lemass remembers seeing her first submarine. Skerries had a particular significance for Lemass. He stayed there with his family before he married Kathleen Hughes, whose family also had a house there. It held happy memories of days spent singing with Jimmy, Ken and Rita O'Dea, in an amateur group which they called the Sandabs.

The war period was to be one of Lemass's busiest. De Valera reshuffled his cabinet to deal with the 'Emergency'. Lemass headed up the new Department of Supplies and Seán MacEntee replaced him in Industry and Commerce but Lemass took back his old portfolio in August 1941 and MacEntee moved to Local Government and Public Health. Gerry Boland became Minister for Justice and Frank Aiken, Minister for the Coordination of Defensive Measures, Oscar Traynor moved to Defence, Seán T. O'Kelly became Minister for Finance and Jim Ryan continued at Agriculture. It was the biggest cabinet reshuffle in the history of the state and was criticised by the opposition as being unwise at such a time of national emergency.

In September 1940 a cabinet committee on internal security was set up and the government drew up plans to rule from a secret location in the event of an invasion. At the beginning of the war the most likely threat to the security of the state came from within rather than without. The IRA stepped up its campaign of violence and the government reacted by interning over 500 activists during the war period. Six were executed during that time. The intelligence service was also concerned about the existence of a pro-Nazi lobby within the IRA. De Valera placed the tough-minded Gerry Boland in Justice to take firm action with the IRA and to deal with the fall-out from unpopular policy decisions. Boland defended his more unpopular decisions and those of the cabinet by insisting that the very existence of the state was under threat.

The government's policy of neutrality did much to strengthen de Valera's isolationist policy, as indeed it did to project him as the leader of nationalist Ireland as a whole. Harold Nicholson held such an opinion of de Valera's standing when he visited Dublin in March 1942. He sensed the popularity of de Valera's stand on neutrality and noted in his diary that on that issue, de Valera exhibited a sense of 'deep spiritual certainty'. Neutrality, Nicholson confided to his diary, had taken on an almost religious flavour, and had become a question of honour, and not something of which Ireland was ashamed. Or as Elizabeth Bowen said, Ireland had 'invested her self-respect in it'.

It was during the war that de Valera gave voice to his private vision of Ireland as a land of 'athletic youths' and – the now

91

legendary – 'comely maidens' in a Saint Patrick's Day speech in 1943:

> The Ireland which we dreamed of would be the home of a people who valued material wealth only as the basis of right living, of a people who were satisfied with frugal comfort and devoted their leisure to things of the spirit – a land whose countryside would be bright with cosy homesteads, whose fields and villages would be joyous with the joy of industry, with the romping of sturdy children, the contests of athletic youths and the laughter of comely maidens, whose fire-sides would be the forums for serene old age.

The war period suited de Valera and his vision admirably. Bew and Patterson observe that he 'found the new atmosphere congenial' and 'moved more and more confidently into the role of philosopher king and idealogue of frugal comfort'. This left Lemass with a more practical role to fill; that of architect to the king. He recognised immediately that even though neutrality was essentially a political matter, it would have serious long-term economic consequences. In an unpublished manuscript for a proposed history of Fianna Fáil, Frank Gallagher notes just how difficult this period was for Lemass and how well he seemed to cope with the task:

> By a combination of care and fearlessness, foresight and drive, he sheltered the Irish people from the worst shortages, and where imported goods could not be got a native substitute was developed and used in its place.

Lemass's private secretary at the Department of Supplies, Pádraic O Slattara, remembered just how difficult the progress of industrial development was in the war years. 'There was nothing in that period in the way of industrial development. We just hung on by our teeth. It was a matter of keeping industries going, such as textiles, for instance, to keep the Army clothed.' Lemass's and the nation's difficulties had to be balanced against the reward of the benefits of neutrality, chief of which was its inextricable link with de Valera's concept of sovereignty.

The crucial question of supplies had been addressed in a series of meetings held by a secret interdepartmental committee of civil servants between 1935 and 1938. Their work was later translated into the well-defined structure of the Department of Supplies. Irish industry was surveyed as to its readiness for an emergency. Lemass found that industrialists were, for the most part, responding positively and were offering to cooperate with the guide-lines his department laid down for the building-up of essential supplies. There were certain exceptions, amongst them the oil distributors who were not especially well-disposed towards Lemass after his efforts to establish an oil refinery in Dublin.

The Federation of Irish Manufacturers and the commercial banks also proved unhelpful at times to the national effort. The former complained about tying money up in an effort to secure additional supplies; the latter were not over-anxious to provide the additional credit required. The Department of Finance proved difficult to convince on the matter of insuring property against war risks. It objected to Lemass's proposals on the basis that they would be seen as an additional tax. He followed the by then familiar path of circumventing MacEntee (still at Finance) by, for example, convincing de Valera of the wisdom of his proposal to reinsure Irish ships with the British Board of Trade.

By 1941, when he held two cabinet portfolios, Lemass's position within the cabinet was supreme. He sat on an economic planning committee of the cabinet which met more than 50 times between 1942 and 1945. It appears from a memorandum from Lemass, circulated in June 1942, that he contemplated the establishment of a permanent ministry to combine the powers he had acquired during the 'Emergency'. He envisaged it as a central planning authority with extensive powers of intervention in the running of the economy. Such a brief had no precedent since the foundation of the state, and the fact that nothing came of it seems to indicate that it met with resistance from the usual cabinet sources. It is unlikely that de Valera would have supported concentrating so much power in the hands of one minister, on such a permanent basis, despite his penchant for delegation. In several Dáil debates de Valera made regular reference to how he saw Lemass's position. He defended the moving of MacEntee into Lemass's department on the basis that the two ministers had been in regular contact over a wide range of issues of common interest to both departments. There was, by that time, what Brian Farrell calls a 'direct endorsement' by de Valera of Lemass's talents. There was no such public endorsement of MacEntee's position and de Valera, as recipient of regular critical memoranda from both parties, was aware of the growing antipathy between two of his most senior ministers. There have been unsubstantiated claims that Lemass considered withdrawing from ministerial office if MacEntee was allowed to continue in Finance. There is no evidence to support this claim apart from a series of sometimes bitter letters and memoranda exchanged between the two ministers which clearly show that Lemass considered MacEntee to be a conservative who slowed up the onward march of his various plans.

Lemass's plan for an all-powerful economic department was not so much a desire for ministerial empire-building on his part, as a genuine wish to centralise economic planning. By the time he had consolidated Supplies and Industry and Commerce under his belt he had developed a very short fuse when it came to criticism either of his policies or his department. He was furious when the *Report of the Commission on Vocational Organisation* criticised the Department of Industry and Commerce. He dismissed the commission's report in the Seanad as 'querulous, nagging, propagandist and a slovenly document'. The commission sat from 1939 to 1943 under the chairmanship of Dr Michael Browne, Bishop of Galway, and it was extremely critical of what it saw as the state's failure to plan properly. This touched a nerve with Lemass. His position, as Professor Joseph Lee has noted, was that while the commission criticized civil servants for doing too much, Lemass criticized them for doing too little. The commission wanted a corporate society, Lemass wanted a corporate state. Browne and Lemass exchanged acrimonious words in the pages of the *Irish*

Press and the report and vocationalism with it, was, in Dermot Keogh's view:

> ...effectively buried in an unmarked grave by the deluge of political and administrative opposition heaped upon it in early 1945. Whatever the temptation might have been for radical political experiment in the 1930s, there was no mainstream political support for a radical change in the structure of the Irish state during the latter months of the war.

Lemass was particularly sensitive to criticism at that time, as his personal life became the subject of the rumour mill. A whispering campaign, orchestrated mostly by the opposition but which also found some support in Fianna Fáil, put it about that Lemass had a serious gambling problem. There were also allegations of corruption in Supplies. It was rumoured at one time that Lemass's gambling debts to one firm of bookmakers in Dublin were so extensive, that a wealthy Dublin businessman and Fianna Fáil supporter, threatened the bookies to ease off Lemass or else he would close them down. No evidence has emerged to support such a claim. Neil Blaney, who is not slow to criticise Lemass on a number of issues, dismissed these claims as nonsense, and points out that even as a minister, Lemass was still receiving financial support from his father, and simply did not have the resources to gamble on a large scale. He did not like being in debt, nor would he entertain the notion of his wife or children being in debt. Lemass was a passionate poker player and took the game very seriously. Family members recall that he would not allow talking at the card table. Peggy Lemass remembers going to the bookies for her father but recalls that the bets he placed were rarely more than one pound or 'if he had a reliable tip, he might risk a fiver'. In relation to the corruption allegations, he told Brian Farrell that to make it clear that his hands were clean he refused to take a single paper from the Supplies ministry when Fianna Fáil lost power in 1948. While Lemass was deeply upset by the allegations he refused to let them direct his attention away from the job at hand. Other allegations, as we shall see, would haunt him later on. But for the present he was more concerned about defining his role in Supplies and said the lies would rebound on the liars.

According to de Valera's description of the Supplies job, Lemass's new portfolio embraced 'the central planning development of our economic life'. It certainly consolidated Lemass's position as the most formidable minister of his generation. Ronan Fanning has assessed the importance of Supplies as the department which, at times even usurped certain prerogatives, which hitherto had been the undisputed preserve of Finance. He also wrote that it:

> played the key role of directing the supply and distribution of agricultural and of manufactured products. As such, it was responsible for co-ordinating and, in practice, directing many of the activities of two other major government departments – Agriculture and Industry and Commerce.

As Minister for Supplies Lemass had unparalleled power over the control of imports, exports and commodity prices. He had complete control over the rationing of consumer goods and in the first four years of the 'Emergency' he made over 600 ministerial orders and informed the nation of the supply situation in regular radio broadcasts. It was at this time he acquired the nickname 'Half-Ounce' Lemass. This war-time soubriquet did not displease him. His administration of the rationing system, which was bedevilled by complexities, won him the admiration of many. Black marketeers were pursued ruthlessly and even some of his own acquaintances did not escape his wrath as he insisted that they be prosecuted. He even took his own mother to task for buying tea on the blackmarket. 'Granny Lemass was not spared his criticism, when he discovered her buying the odd pound of tea on the black market', his daughter Maureen recalls. She also recalls that the quality of food in their house was no better than might be found in any household at the time. 'There was one unfortunate incident when the deer in the Phoenix Park were slaughtered to provide meat', she remembers, 'and my father received one, but because we knew nothing about how venison should be hung, the meat was rotten by the time we came to eat it.'

To show cause with those who were unable to get petrol supplies, he abandoned his ministerial car and took to using a bicycle. His only complaint was that the muscles in his legs were not up to the task.

Professor James Meenan has made the point that in his handling of the rationing system, Lemass often concealed the strength of his hand. He prepared the country for the worst, but since the worst never quite came, everybody put up with a great deal because they had been prepared by Lemass to put up with so much more. Despite the introduction of compulsory tillage in 1940 there were severe food shortages. Bread was rationed from 1942, as was sugar and tea. Coal, gas and petrol were in very short supply and private motoring was replaced across the country with horsedrawn carriages, carts and makeshift trailers. To foreigners however, Dublin seemed like a land of plenty, with beef available for those who could afford it, and the restaurants of the Irish capital still able to rise to presentable fare. Some remarked on the 'gaiety' of the city and noted that the 'Emergency' gave it an international atmosphere that it lacked since before the Act of Union. Others saw it as a city where the poor ran the risk of scurvy and rickets from the lack of a properly balanced diet. It was Lemass's brief to see that such horrors be avoided.

His unorthodox approach to running the Supplies ministry came in for a certain amount of criticism from the opposition. He posed problems of nightmarish proportion for civil servants accustomed to a more leisurely pace. He insisted that all enquiries to the department be answered within a week and this often proved taxing for staff, due to the large number of personal callers, letters and telephone enquiries arriving daily at the department. If an enquiry lingered longer than two weeks, the minister took a very poor view of it. In short, usual bureaucratic methods were jettisoned in favour of a formula devised by Lemass. The powers which Lemass had at his disposal were considerable; they covered wage control, restrictions on emigration and even withdrawal of unemployment assistance.

To help him administer this regime Lemass brought John Leydon with him from Industry and Commerce. A survey of the department by those who worked there reflects their view of his methods:

> During the emergency period serious problems often arose which had to be solved immediately....It became the accepted policy that it was better...to take some action quickly (even if later experience was to suggest modifications) than to attempt to find the perfect solution by waiting until all the facts had been ascertained...*ad hoc* schemes for distribution and tentative solutions of problems adopted at an early stage had often to be altered. Nevertheless, experience showed that the policy was a wise one and that the surest way of finding the flaws in any scheme was to put it in operation.

As the course of the war advanced, the Department of Supplies in effect provided a tailor-made institutional setting in which Lemass could reassess his approach to economic policy. His thinking was influenced, but not totally transformed, by the wartime experience. Three significant areas stand out. His commitment to his policy of self-sufficiency was reinforced when the benefits of the 1938 Trade Agreement with Britain were suspended and when neutrality increased Ireland's isolation. That commitment was reaffirmed at the Fianna Fáil Árd Fheis of 1943. Lemass was now more firmly convinced than ever of the need for state intervention to bolster development. He also looked afresh at certain weaknesses in the Irish business community which he earmarked as stays on the development of industry.

During the war years Lemass was a close observer of policy shifts in Britain. In this he was unique amongst his cabinet colleagues.

In April 1941 he and the Minister for Agriculture, Jim Ryan, held talks in London with a view to having British restrictions on supplies to Ireland eased. The British entrenched stand on Irish neutrality and Churchill's nomination as prime minister made the conclusion of a new agreement next to impossible.

At a time when he was charged with the task of finding a solution to the unemployment crisis, Lemass was particularly influenced by the publication of the *Beveridge Report* in Britain. The report sparked further disagreement between Lemass and MacEntee, this time on the approach to post-war planning. Lemass's integrationist approach is evident from a speech made in 1943 when he stated the government was committed 'to end involuntary unemployment...'

> Its solution will be found if we get a new conception of their responsibility by the state, employers and trade union movement. Unemployment is mainly a symptom of defective industrial organisation. It is not an inevitable feature of an economy based on private enterprise or organised on democratic lines.

Of all the state enterprises developed by Lemass when Minister for Supplies, one of the most significant was Irish Shipping. Cordial arrangements were agreed at the beginning of the war whereby British shipping allocated space for Irish supplies but this arrangement lasted a short period. American policy on neutrality prevented her ships from entering Irish ports and the supply of vessels available for charter began to dry up. The situation became desperate. Lemass established Irish Shipping in March 1941 with J.F. Dempsey as secretary.

Lemass and Leydon sent scouts world-wide to find anything capable of floating.

The first foreign ship to join the fleet was a Greek vessel, the *Vassilios Destounis* which had been found as a wreck in the Spanish port of Avilés. She had been the victim of a German air attack and was salvaged by Spanish fishermen after being abandoned by her crew. The mainmast collapsed when the Irish crew attempted to load her with grain, and the engines failed on the first leg of the journey home. Nevertheless she reached Dublin and was renamed the *Irish Poplar*. Several ships which had been abandoned by their owners in Irish ports at the outbreak of war were commandeered and compensation was paid to their owners later. Refurbishing work was done in Cork and with the aid of money borrowed from the banks, Lemass put 15 ships on the high seas. Hardly an impressive fleet, but it gave a considerable morale boost to a country trying to maintain a difficult supplies situation. The ships were said to be a danger to convoys because they travelled so slowly, so they often travelled alone at night, brightly flood-lit, flying the tricolour and with the words EIRE in huge letters painted on the side of their hulls. Though it had such humble and inauspicious origins, Irish Shipping came out of the war with a surplus in hand of around £3,000,000 and only two of its ships lost.

Lemass had a number of legislative concerns which occupied his attention completely apart from the supplies situation. He steered the Children's Allowances Bill through the Dáil and Seanad. Lemass had pushed for an early decision on the allowances but had to wait two and a half years before the legislation progressed from planning to enactment. Again MacEntee was in the first rank of objectors to the proposed introduction on non-means tested children's allowances and dole, his objections vacillating between the moral and the practical.

Another piece of legislation, the Transport Bill, provided Lemass with an opportunity to outline some of his concerns in the area of post-war planning, when he introduced the measure to the Dail on 2 May 1944:

> The government contemplates that the immediate post-war situation will be one of critical significance in the future economic development of the country. It is our view that we should get ourselves organised now in every important economic sphere to face the problems and to avail of the opportunities which the post-war period may bring. Our national economic development requires that our public services, including our transport services, should be thoroughly efficient. It requires also that they should be self-supporting....Whatever theoretical case may be made for competition in encouraging efficiency or stimulating enterprise in other economic spheres, it can, in relation to

transport, undermine the stability of the services which are necessary to the national commercial life and it can, in its effect, do irreparable damage, to the public interest....Our national economic efficiency, our competitive effectiveness in inter-national trade, depend not merely upon the actual charges for public transport in operation but upon the total of the overhead burden that industry and agriculture must carry....We have in recent years extended state ownership or state regulation in the economic field to a considerable extent...we have experimented with different types of organisation...the aim of the government in devising methods of controlling these various concerns was, first of all, to ensure that the government would have control in matters of general policy and, secondly, to see that these concerns should have complete freedom in matters of day-to-day management, but particularly to see that such concerns would be free from anything in the way of political pressure....The government has never been satisfied that it has yet devised a satisfactory organisation or method for the carrying out of that type of enterprise.

This is a revealing speech in the Lemass canon and has some of the principal elements of his thinking in the war period and beyond. Much of what he is saying indicates that while he was keen to make advances in policy matters, he was still influenced by his thinking of the 1930s, continuity and not radical change, was still the order of the day. His firm commitment to protection remained in place, though it was supplemented by a more active export drive. There was, as yet, no major concession to the international agencies, to deficit spending or to expansionary budgets.

Brian Girvin, in his superb account of the period, *Between Two Worlds: Politics and Economy in Independent Ireland*, says that Lemass, despite his appreciation and understanding of the new economics, was forced by post-war circumstances to continue his older policies. 'When faced with the choice between the uncertaintity of innovation', Dr Girvin writes, 'and the certainties of what was in place, he chose the latter....At policy level, as distinct from some general remarks made at the time, the objectives of Industry and

Commerce do not depart on any point of substance from the certainties established during the 1930s.' This view is supported by a speech to the students at Bolton Street College, Dublin, on 19 November 1944, in which he expressed the view that post-war plans, in themselves, did not represent the key to prosperity. 'The emphasis', he told the Literary and Debating Society, 'must be put, not so much on plans, as on increased production by hard work, if we are to expand the national income and achieve prosperity.' Lemass told the students he wanted to see the emphasis 'not so much on post-war planning as on production, increased production per man hour, per acre, per machine, per skilled worker, and hard work'. A former Labour TD from Cork, James Hickey, criticised this view because he felt Lemass failed to give the trade union movement an active role in the areas he was preaching about. James Larkin junior, noted that Lemass was moving away from what he saw as his former 'socialist outlook' towards the interests of 'private ownership and private control'. What Lemass was really doing, was reining in the rising expectations of a people who desperately wanted a rise in living standards.

The immediate post-war situation offered little hope of that. In December 1945 the unemployment figure stood at over 70,000. It was expected to rise radically with the return of war workers and demobbed soldiers from Britain. That did not occur, the reverse was the case, as hoards of Irish workers took the emigration route to the major industrial cities of England.

An already grave situation was exacerbated by the failure of the harvest of 1946. Lemass had to reintroduce the rationing of bread. Food subsidies were introduced but taxes were raised to pay for them. Butter and fuel were also rationed, so it seemed to the population, who were just coming out of one emergency, that they were entering another. The period was marked by high unemployment, growing emigration and continuous balance of payments' deficits all of which led to widespread dissatisfaction.

It is worth noting the official Fianna Fáil version of the post-war years, published in 1960 and endorsed by Lemass:

> Very different conditions faced the Fianna Fáil government in the post-war years. An impoverished world, shortages of machinery and materials and inflated currencies were big obstacles to the resumption of national progress, but planning and preparations went on. The defence forces were demobilised and work found as far as possible for the members. And as the trickle of raw materials and machinery increased, the advance was resumed. By 1947 the worst effects had passed...plans for industrial expansion and agricultural development, carefully prepared by the Fianna Fáil government during the emergency years, were beginning to be put into operation. Suddenly, in 1948, a political move of an unusual kind brought down the government and destroyed the atmosphere of stability, confidence and progress so carefully fostered over the years.

And it is worth contrasting with that view, the opinion of the late Provost of Trinity, F.S.L. Lyons, on how he saw Ireland after she emerged from her neutral state at war's end:

> The tensions and the liberations of war, the shared experience, the comaradeship in suffering, the new thinking about the future, all these things had passed her by. It was as if an entire people had been condemned to live in Plato's cave, backs to the fire of life and deriving their only knowledge of what went on outside from the flickering shadows thrown on the wall before their eyes by the men and women who passed to and fro behind them. When after six years they emerged dazzled, from the cave into the light of day, it was to a new and vastly different world.

A review of Lemass's position at the end of the war shows the obvious success he made of the Supplies department, on the one hand, balanced against a number of failures, albeit not of his own making, on the other. He was presiding over a small, open economy which was extremely vulnerable to outside influences and heavily dependant on its trading with its nearest neighbour. Most of the proposals which Lemass put forward during the war years were steamrolled by de Valera and his conservative and ageing cabinet. Lemass's proposal for a particular type of economic planning committee, which would be a major planning force, received a hasty rejection. His proposal for a Ministry of Labour which would galvanise Irish labour policy was also rejected by de Valera, who cautioned his minister to 'make haste slowly' on such matters. He recommended an overhaul of the tax system so as to provide the 'maximum inducement to industrialists to accumulate funds for the replacement of obsolete plant'. He also advocated the setting up of a state export board to help market Irish goods abroad and he recommended the establishment of industries to service that market.

In his Full Employment Memorandum he proposed that budget deficits be provided for and he also proposed that banking structures and government policy should work in tandem.

The majority of his major proposals fell on deaf ears. Tim Pat Coogan has noted that de Valera rarely confronted Lemass head on. His method was to 'smother Lemass in the general web of a deeply conservative cabinet's disapproval'. De Valera was anxious to rein Lemass in and he left it to people like MacEntee to do the dirty work for him. This had been evident from the very early days of the party when Lemass was viewed as the hatchetman and had made a speech which brought the odium of the old guard down on his head. He suggested it was time to leave behind the old rhetoric and move on. A call went up for him to be disciplined. A heated all-night debate ensued and de Valera never once stepped in to save Lemass's hide. His silence was a clear indication that he did not disapprove of Lemass's wings being clipped. Joseph Lee sums up the relationship between the two perceptively: 'Mr de Valera, for his part, had to combine encouragement with restraint; Mr Lemass had to fuse deference with decisiveness. The skill with which Mr de Valera harnessed the energies of a potentially difficult colleague was not the least of his successes in man-management.'

Government Secretary, Maurice Moynihan, who worked with de Valera and Lemass told Tim Pat Coogan that he often wondered about the relationship between de Valera and Lemass. 'Lemass was very un-Irish', he said, 'he had the Huguenot strain in him. He was very determined, confident in himself, hard-working. Lemass barked a lot. He fought continuously with MacEntee in cabinet. Dev was reluctant to interfere at all.' When asked to describe the relationship, Neil Blaney said 'it would be easier to describe the relationship between God and the Holy Ghost'.

When de Valera expanded the economic planning committee, in April 1945, to include the whole cabinet, any hope Lemass had of implementing his plans was firmly knocked on the head. As a result the years ahead were a particularly stagnant time for the Irish economy.

Within a few weeks of the war's conclusion Fianna Fáil faced a major electoral test. Seán T. O'Kelly, a loyal but at times difficult de Valera supporter and regular thorn in Lemass's side, was chosen to stand for the presidency. He stood against General Seán MacEoin, a former army chief of staff and a man Lemass had little respect for. The other candidate was independent republican Patrick McCartan. Lemass attacked MacEoin for his Blueshirt past and said the Fine Gael candidate had voted against the 1937 Constitution and favoured the retention of the trappings of national subjection. He claimed the anti-Irish foreign press was supporting MacEoin. Voting took place on 14 June and O'Kelly succeeded Douglas Hyde as President of Ireland. Dr Hyde wrote to Lemass before leaving office:

> As I am coming to the end of my term as President of Ireland, I would not like to go without saying good-bye to you and at the same time thanking you for the co-operation and kindness which you always accorded to me. I am sending you a little book of my own poems and I would be greatly honoured if you would accept it as a token of my esteem for you.

Fianna Fáil had been in power for 13 consecutive years and the complacency which attends such constant exercise of power was beginning to show. There were difficult years ahead for the party.

For Lemass, now the mature cabinet minister, another step up the political ladder followed O'Kelly's election to the presidency. De Valera chose him to replace O'Kelly as Tánaiste [deputy Prime Minister] and with that appointment began his period of waiting in the wings to succeed de Valera, a time which Neil Blaney described as the party's period of wondering 'not so much when Lemass would take over, but when Dev would go'.

Lemass's status, as mature and influential cabinet minister had received international recognition before de Valera nominated him as Tánaiste. Just before he became Tánaiste the Vatican conferred one of its most prestigious honours on him. The Papal Nuncio, Mgr Paschal Robinson wrote to inform him, on 4 May, that the Pope had decided to award him The Grand Cross of the Order of St Gregory The Great, in recognition of his work for the relief of distressed areas in Europe during the war.

Honoured abroad and revered at home, Lemass, who had served apprenticeships as distinct as hatter and government minister, now began to serve yet another apprenticeship – that of leader in waiting.

9

OPPOSITION ONCE AGAIN

1948 was a year Seán Lemass dearly wished to blot from his memory. There were three principal reasons for this. He emerged exonerated but scarred from a financial scandal; his second daughter Peggy spent most of the year in hospital being treated for tuberculosis; and Fianna Fáil lost power.

Peggy said the seriousness of her illness caused her father grave upset. He placed her in the Mater Private Hospital which he could not afford, and the medical bills added severe strain to an already financially overstretched household. Lemass supported three children at expensive private schools and at university and maintained his own lifestyle as a public representative on his political salary which was never enough to make ends meet. His father often helped out when things got particularly difficult. Things became so difficult in 1948 that he borrowed what was then the enormous sum of £1,000, from the National City Bank, to cover the year's medical expenses arising from his daughter's illness.

The financial scandal concerned the sale of the Locke distillery in Kilbeggan, County Weastmeath. It was a complex affair. The company secretary bid unsuccessfully for the company. A curious cocktail of continental businessmen, including at least one wanted on criminal charges in England, also tried for a takeover. The sale was an embarrassment to Lemass because his department had been approached before the sale about the enlargement of the company's export quota. The government was also embarrassed because President Seán T. O'Kelly entertained some of the more criminal element of the consortium in Áras an Uachtaráin and the occasion was reported in the press. Oliver J. Flanagan, with the benefit of parliamentary privilege, made political capital out of the affair in the Dáil on 22,

29 and 30 of October 1947, casting allegations in all directions. De Valera, his son Eamon, Gerry Boland and Lemass were all targeted as being corrupt. De Valera established a tribunal to investigate the allegations and after 18 days sitting it cleared the parties of the alleged corruption charges made by Flanagan. The tribunal came down strongly on Flanagan, a former Independent who had joined Fine Gael, accusing him of 'complete irresponsibility'. There was not even a scintilla of evidence to suggest that Lemass benefited in any way from the sale but the sulphur of suspicion was heavy in the air. It did not dissipate quickly, as two other tribunals investigated claims that a parliamentary secretary, Dr F.C. Ward, was involved in shady dealings in relation to the sale of a bacon factory in Monaghan and that members of Fianna Fáil, including Lemass, were involved in stock exchange manipulation. But again while the charges did not stick Lemass felt damaged by the rumours.

Seán O'Faoláin's description of the post-war situation might well apply to Lemass's mood in 1948:

> We emerge, a little dulled, bewildered, deflated. There is a great leeway to make up, many lessons to be learned, problems to be solved which, in those six years of silence, we did not even allow ourselves to state.

To make up some of that post-war leeway, Lemass considered a series of proposals to increase industrial efficiency. These proposals indicated the level of his disillusion with the performance of Irish industry and its failure to serve the needs of the economy except under compulsion. Industrial growth needed to be stimulated. Lemass sought the establishment of a Foreign Trade Corporation in March 1946 with the aim of encouraging exports. He abandoned that proposal within the year due mainly to the fact that he considered the international economic climate to be unpropitious. It was replaced in October 1947 with a plan to establish a Trade Advisory Council which would advise and grant-aid exporters. This later proposal met with the disapproval of Finance and Lemass was still embroiled in a row with the department over the proposals, when the government fell. Had Fianna Fáil stayed in power in 1948 his proposals were unlikely to have gone beyond the planning stage. Aware of this he drew up another strategy which, though less impressive and on the face of it more conservative, met with an avalanche of criticism. The measure was the Industrial Efficiency Bill.

In 1946 Lemass had called for extensive powers of intervention including the power of compulsory acquisition of companies by the state. 'Business transferred' was how Lemass saw such acquisition; 'commandeered industry' was how Finance saw it. The Minister for Finance held the view that under the legislation the ownership of capital would be diminished to the level of trusteeship. It was not surprising that a major furore followed the announcement of the package. Industrialists were up in arms. Even the hostility which Lemass had faced down in 1946 when he established the Labour Court paled into insignificance with the fury that was now unleashed on him. Not surprisingly the *Irish Independent* did not back Lemass's proposals but he did find support in an editorial of *The Irish Times* on 1 October 1947 which correctly predicted the outcry from the business community:

> Some of our native industries are as efficient as anybody could expect them to be; but others are not. It is against these others that the more drastic provisions of the Bill are aimed....certain manufacturers in this country have been waxing fat on profits which have been the direct outcome of protective tariffs.

The Federation of Irish Manufacturers, using its president P.J. Kavanagh, as its mouthpiece, raised the old chestnut of communism in criticising Lemass:

> No one...would say that Mr Lemass was a Communist, but it would have to be admitted that he was flirting with Communistic ideals in his Efficiency Bill. The rights and privileges of private enterprise were, in this bill, challenged very seriously.

It is hardly surprising that the cabinet invited Lemass to redraw his proposals on industrial efficiency. The revisions included the establishment of development councils in industry, which proposed a role for workers in structuring the way industry was run. Lemass was on a sticky wicket and he knew it. The provisions of the bill were an important indicator for the future but the initiatives remained in embryonic form, awaiting birth, until Lemass became Taoiseach. The revised bill reached a second reading on 8 October 1947 but lapsed when the Dáil was dissolved. Fine Gael introduced a number of amendments to the bill with a view to delaying rather than improving it. The bill also raised its head during the rather long and drawn out 1948 election campaign, when it was used by Fine Gael as a stick to beat the government. With 15 months of the government's term still to run, de Valera, worried by a number of things, mostly by the rise of Clann na Poblachta, decided on a snap general election.

Of three by-elections held in October 1947, Clann na Poblachta won two. This was in sharp contrast to Fianna Fáil's victory in four of the six by-elections held in 1945-6. Seán MacBride beat Fianna Fáil stalwart Tommy Mullins to a seat in Dublin County. But a more serious blow to morale was the election of the Clann's Paddy Kinane in Tipperary. Both candidates received fewer first preference votes than their Fianna Fáil rivals but won on transfers from other opposition parties. Before the by-elections de Valera warned that if his government was weakened he would call a general election. Relying for the most part on his own judgement he called it for February 1948. Lemass later claimed that de Valera consulted him on the calling of the election and he advised his leader to go to the country. However had he advised otherwise, it seems unlikely that de Valera would have changed his mind. He was truly perturbed about the ground being gained by Clann na Poblachta and the by-election victories can only have confirmed him in that view. Even the party's name must have given Fianna Fáil cause for reflection – it has been interpreted to mean 'Family or Party of the Republic' and even 'Republican Party'. Its leadership had solid republican credentials. At its inaugural meeting in Dublin on 6 July 1946, Seán MacBride, former IRA Chief of Staff, was elected leader. As the son of Maud Gonne and Major Seán MacBride he could claim a distinguished republican lineage. As a barrister he represented top IRA men in court on a very regular basis.

What did the Clann stand for? It was clearly anti-Fianna Fáil. One of the Executive's early statements talked about 'the low standard of political morality set up by those who in the name of republicanism entered office'. It said it was concerned about the lot of the worker – low wages, unemployment and inflation. It was also concerned not to be identified as communist or unconstitutional. Fianna Fáil identified it as having communist leanings. During the general election campaign of 1948 the Executive of the Clann was kept busy with damage limitation exercises aimed at avoiding the party's being tarred with the red brush. Seán MacEntee said the party contained members who belonged to organisations disapproved of by the Catholic Church and Erskine Childers accused the Clann of having a fascist philosophy. De Valera dismissed their policies as irrelevant. MacBride rushed more to the defence of the membership's ideology than to his party's policies. The members were, he said, 'nationalist, Catholic and Christian'. The political scientist, Peter Mair, describes the party as one which sought to 'marry republican discontent, and a strong commitment to social justice, in a replication in miniature of the earlier Fianna Fáil appeal'.

The Fianna Fáil government of the immediate post-war period was for the most part complacent. Sixteen years of continuous power quite naturally gave a sense of false security. Lemass's interventionist policies in the period fell victim to that complacency. Lemass himself, like his cabinet colleagues, thought that there was no real alternative to Fianna Fáil in 1948. And, like his cabinet colleagues, he was not prepared for the loss of power.

Clann na Poblachta nominated 93 candidates at the '48 election; only Fianna Fáil nominated more. In an attempt to stymie the Clann, de Valera introduced the Electoral

(Amendment) Bill 1947, which was little more than a calculated attempt to gerrymander the constituencies. There had been calls for an all-party committee on the revision of the constituencies, to prevent what William Norton called 'hoofling', but that call was ignored. Clann na Poblachta's success in the local elections in June 1947 was a far more elegant call for constituency revision, in de Valera's mind, than anything the Labour leader might have to say on the subject. The number of Dáil seats remained static at 138 since 1935. De Valera increased the number to 147 despite the fact that the population had fallen. More significantly, the number of three-seat constituencies was increased from 15 to 22, a move which would not benefit the smaller parties. Various arguments were advanced to defend the revision but none was convincing.

Clann na Poblachta fought a vigorous campaign promising to admit Northern Ireland MPs to the Dáil; giving farmers greater control over agricultural policy; and offering 'idealism' as an alternative to Fianna Fáil's 'political patronage'. Most political commentators felt the party would do well. Its own pundits predicted it could take as many as 75 seats. In the end it took only ten, being defeated by the cruel mathematical sophistry of proportional representation, having achieved the third highest number of votes cast in the election. Fine Gael won 31 seats, Labour 14, National Labour 5, Clann na Talmhan 7, Independents 12. Fianna Fáil lost 8, retaining 68 seats in a parliament of 147. Clann na Poblachta joined in an inter-party government in which it got two ministries; Seán MacBride became Minister for External Affairs and Dr Noel Browne became Minister for Health.

Erskine Childers, a future Tánaiste and President, offered this view of Fianna Fáil's defeat in a letter to MacEntee, just after the election:

Our TDs were careless, shockingly briefed and a very large number contented themselves with talking up Dev and down with coalition....We underestimated the Clann....We underestimated F.G. There are 250,000 voters of age 21 to 25 who do not believe there is any substantial difference between us and F.G. They chose F.F. because of Dev and other personalities. There is in fact no policy difference save on the Irish language.

Childers was one of the very few Fianna Fáil TDs who saw the writing on the wall and talked openly to colleagues about the need for the party to take a new direction. He said people were tired of the 'old faces' who had given great service but had become 'inarticulate between elections'. He was concerned that even in defeat the party might remain complacent and think of the 1948 débâcle in the terms in which it was described by Trinity academic and Labour Party member David Thornley in 1963, when he wrote that Fianna Fáil endured defeat in 1948 'as a manifestation of popular folly and ingratitude much as Jehovah endured the periodic deviation of the Israelites'. Fianna Fáil had fought the election with the slogan 'Play Safe'. The electorate, in the party's view, had chosen to play dangerously.

Lemass own view as the results were announced was that:

> ...we did not think we had lost the election...the National Labour Party had fought the election on the basis that they were going to support a Fianna Fáil government....Up to the night before the Dáil met we did not realise there was going to be a majority against us.

According to de Valera's official biographers, Longford and O'Neill, right up to the hour the Dáil met, there was no guarantee that a coalition was certain:

> Even on the day when the Dáil assembled a coalition seemed far from certain. De Valera understood up to a short time before the meeting that National Labour refused to participate. Then he was told that agreement had been reached. There was a hustle to prepare his office for his departure. His papers had to be gathered up hurriedly.

Brian Farrell sums up Lemass's situation after the election thus:

> ...after sixteen years in government he was out of office, for a
> very broad anti-Fianna Fáil coalition was formed and secured
> a majority under John A. Costello. He could look back over
> the two decades of of parliamentary endeavour to a record of
> extraordinary achievement. The young gunman turned
> politician had become the most accomplished ministerial
> craftsman of his generation. The man who had done so
> much to create Fianna Fáil was now its deputy leader. He
> seemed poised, at the height of his considerable powers, to
> take the next step forward and upward in his political career.

There would, however, be a ten-year wait before Lemass took that
step. In the short term he had to adjust to being in opposition
again. As with all government ministers who lose office, the first
most tangible loss is that of the state car. His daughter Maureen
remembers her father being driven home in his official car and
then having to borrow his son Noel's car to get him into Dublin
the next day. He later purchased a modest Ford in which he
drove his children about the countryside on motoring trips.
Peggy says her father was more relaxed than when in office and
it was at this time they got to know him better as a father. She
recalled that during the war the nuns at Muckross Park, where
she was at school, asked her to intercede with her father for food
supplies for the school. She could only apologise and refuse,
offering the excuse that she was not in a position to make such a
request because she did not know her father very well. That
situation changed in 1948. His daughters recall their father
telling them that he was unlikely ever to be in a position to leave
them money, so he promised them what he considered to be
something even more valuable, an education. Peggy and
Maureen both attended UCD where Maureen met her future
husband, Charles Haughey who was introduced to her by Harry
Boland, son of Lemass's colleague Gerry Boland.

The Lemass daughters also remember that, like most fathers,
theirs took a particular interest in the type of boyfriend they

brought home. Peggy said he was happy with her decision to marry an army officer, Jack O'Brien, who later became his ADC. Sheila said he was relieved when she married businessman John O'Connor, because her mother and father both liked the genial pipe smoker, and, as her sisters said, because the Lemass's thought him the most suitable of all her boyfriends. The family recall that he had an excellent relationship with the young Charles Haughey who, though renowned for his precociousness, was always reserved in the presence of his father-in-law. Lemass's only son, Noel, married Eileen Delaney, who trained as an actress with the Abbey School of Acting. She stood in the Dublin South-West by-election caused by the death of her husband in 1976. Eileen Lemass was elected to the Dáil in 1977. Noel Lemass was a deputy for Dublin south city constituencies for 20 years. He was first elected at a by-election in 1956 and joined his father in the Dáil. He was Parliamentary Secretary [Minister for State] at Finance from 1969 to 1973.

Most commentators agree that this period in opposition, 1948-51, was a fallow time for Lemass. He was dismayed to see the Department of External Affairs, under Seán MacBride, take on certain aspects of the innovatory role that was traditionally the reserve of Industry and Commerce. MacBride, because of his pivotal position in the coalition, was allowed greater freedom to dabble in economic affairs than was the usual practice for a minister with a non-economic portfolio. Further cause for Lemass's dismay was the fact that his old post was in the hands of Dan Morrissey, a Fine Gael TD from Tipperary, who had once been deputy leader of Labour, but crossed the floor of the House in 1933 to join Fine Gael. When appointing Morrissey, Costello informed him that he was giving him the 'toughest job of the lot'. Lemass had little regard for Morrissey and the feeling was entirely mutual. 'I won't say I liked Lemass', Morrissey told *The Irish Times* as late as 1980. On 12 May 1948 Lemass offered this view of Morrissey to William Dywer, of Seafield Fabrics, Youghal, County Cork, who had just met the new minister:

I am not surprised that your interview with Morrissey was unsatisfactory. He does not seem to have made up his mind as to where he is going in the matter of industrial development, and others have had the same experience as yourself. My personal view is that he will neither remove any existing protective duties or recommend any new ones.

It is clear from the carping that the two men engaged in across the floor of the Dáil that Lemass clearly saw Morrissey as his inferior, and that his presence in Industry and Commerce merely devalued his old department. Lemass also disliked him because, during the 'Emergency', he led the opposition in the Dáil to the amalgamation of Supplies and Industry and Commerce under Lemass's stewardship.

Morrissey lacked ministerial experience, and nowhere was this more evident than in his relations with his civil servants. The raw recruit to ministerial power lacked the skill to deal with his officials and he is remembered as taking the 'bull in the china shop approach' with even the most senior civil servants in Industry and Commerce. Lemass was annoyed when Morrissey put himself forward as the champion of protection. In a speech in the United States in 1949 he advocated a strong protectionist policy which harped back to the days of the 1930s. It irritated, not just Lemass, but also the Tánaiste and Labour leader, William Norton, who always had serious reservations about protectionist policies, and alleged on several occasions, that the 'fat cats' of industry were the ones who benefited most from protectionist tariffs.

Curiously, for one who was held in not especially high regard, within or outside the cabinet, it was Dan Morrissey who has to his credit the establishment of the Industrial Development Authority. Its brief was wide, and on the face of it, it seemed tailor-made to develop much of what Lemass had been seeking to promote since the end of the war. The IDA was established to 'advise and assist the government in the intensification of industrial development on the best possible lines'.

It seems especially odd that it was Lemass's voice that was raised most loudly in objection to the establishment of the new authority. Lemass's arguments against Morrissey's IDA are far from convincing and it is difficult to believe that he accepted them himself. Bew and Patterson advance the reason for his disapproval as having much to do with what he saw as a downgrading of his beloved Industry and Commerce. There was considerable resistance amongst senior officials in the department to the proposal. Bew and Patterson also stress that the establishment of the IDA was a victory for Lemass's old department over the traditionalists in Finance. The coalition Finance Minister, Patrick McGilligan, was anxious that the IDA should not be 'a gang of crack-pot socialistic planners'. As soon as the government announced its plans for the IDA on 12 February 1949, Lemass engaged in attack. He had fallen out of favour with certain elements of big business in the wake of the industrial efficiency debate. They were supporters of Fianna Fáil and it was expedient that a certain amount of fence-mending needed to be done. The IDA debate provided Lemass with that much-needed opportunity. He condemned the proposal as 'anti-industrial' and he said 'Irish industry is being asked to show its merit by wining the race for increased productivity dragging a cart – a cart without wheels'. He accused the government of being hostile to industrial profits. What the debate really shows is that Lemass had not adjusted to being in opposition, or more realistically, being out of power.

In opposition he continued to advise industrialists who sought his opinion. One such was William Dwyer of Cork with whom he had regular correspondence between 1948 to 1951. On 19 December 1950 Lemass wrote Dwyer a letter in which he made a strong attack on the Labour leader:

Industry as a whole will have to defend itself against the stupid attacks of Norton and the rest of the political tribe who are trying to divert public criticism of their own incompetence by directing it against the industrialists.

In the same letter he took up the issue of industrial development:

> ...the extent to which industrial development is to be brought, must be decided by national policy and not by the interests of individual industrialists. It has always been a handicap to our industrial progress that the best of our industrial leaders show a tendency to exhaust early their initial impetus and to slow down and stop when they have reached a stage of development which gives them maximum security with the minimum of additional effort ....The function of Government as I see it is to keep on pushing development to the limits of practicability whether individual industrialists like it or not.

Lemass felt that the coalition government failed to push industrial development to the limits he wished to see in place.

In the popular mind the inter-party government is best remembered, not for its industrial policy, but for two very unrelated issues; the declaration of a republic, by John A. Costello in Canada and Noel Browne's Mother and Child Scheme which brought the administration down. Lemass was more involved with the former.

Costello's decision to declare a republic in Ottawa on 7 September 1948 remains one of the more bewildering episodes in recent Irish history. The ground has been gone over by historians and political writers many times, yet it remains something of an enigma. Some support the view that Costello had the backing of the cabinet, others, including Noel Browne, claim that he had no such support. F.H. Boland who drafted Costello's address to the Canadian lawyers recalled that nothing whatsoever in the speech referred to the External Relations Act. The repeal of the Act, announced at such distance, was certainly news back in Dublin. MacBride heard about it while dining in the Russell Hotel, officials in External Affairs heard about it from journalists looking for comment. Fianna Fáil's view was essentially that Costello had done the right thing in the wrong way. De Valera held with the view that the way in which the republic was declared led to a strengthening of partition. In London Clement Attlee's government determined that Ireland would continue to enjoy Commonwealth privileges. The bad news from London was that the Ireland Act of 1949 declared that 'in no event will Northern Ireland or any part thereof cease to be part of His Majesty's Dominions and of the United Kingdom without the consent of the parliament of Northern Ireland'. The whole episode was what Dermot Keogh has called 'a perfect example of the triumph of the politics of muddle'.

Lemass delivered a long speech on the repeal of the External Relations Act in the Dáil on 24 and 25 November 1948 in which he said:

> I do not think it is suffficient to say that the enactment of this measure will tend to promote peace and concord amongst our people or 'remove the gun out of Irish politics'. That is a phrase I do not like. It is a phrase that will be quoted abroad to belittle this country. I do not think it is true to say that the gun has been in Irish politics – certainly not for a quarter of a century.

Lemass told Brian Farrell in a private interview that he had urged de Valera to repeal the External Relations Act because he was of the opinion that Irish neutrality during the war might have been compromised by the ambiguity of the Act. We have the word of F.H. Boland to support the view that de Valera would have kept Ireland in the Commonwealth but would have rid the Act of all references to the Crown. It is not the view that the average member of Fianna Fáil would have held, but Dr Boland recalled de Valera telling Churchill in 1953 that if he had remained head of government he would have retained the Commonwealth link.

As the debate on the repeal of the External Relations Act raged Lemass entered into a long correspondence with Captain Henry Harrison, the 82 year-old President of the Paddington Branch of the Anti-Partition of Ireland League. Captain Harrison came to the attention of the British public when he was referred to in the House of Lords on 23 May 1949 by the Marquess of Salisbury.

Harrison sent Lemass a copy of a sample amendment he had drafted to the Ireland Bill, copies of which he had circulated to MPs of all parties. He proposed to delete the words 'without the consent of the Parliament of Northern Ireland' and substitute the words 'without the consent of the people of Northern Ireland ascertained by plebiscite properly conducted in accordance with true democratic principles...'.

Harrison's colours can be judged from the reason he offered for the indispensability of the amendment. He saw the Parliament of Northern Ireland as an 'instrument of a tyrannical Ascendancy which is used to perpetuate that Ascendancy by legislative and administrative chicanery, by mob terrorism supported by police oppression – exactly as the Nazi Brown Shirts were supported by the several police forces under Himmler and Germany'.

Offering such views to MPs can only have reduced Harrison's effectiveness as a lobbyist. One Liberal MP was reminded in a letter from Harrison that the date on which he was writing was the sixty-seventh anniversary of the Phoenix Park murders. On the police in Northern Ireland he wrote: 'No police system ever devised can wholly suppress the protesting indignation of our Irish patriots.'

Harrison told Lemass that anti-partitionists in London were disappointed with the way the inter-party government had declared the republic. He claimed in a letter to Lemass of 16 June 1949 that the 'coalition of incompatibles' as he called the Irish government, did a deal with the British which would allow some sort of federal relationship between the Republic of Ireland and Northern Ireland, but he claimed the Irish 'baulked at going through with their part in the intrigue'. Harrison was a believer in conspiracy theories. He told Lemass in the same letter that he had been contacted by the historian Nicholas Mansergh but he was suspicious of such a contact because of Mansergh's contacts with British officialdom. He forwarded the communication to Lemass and requested that they be passed on to de Valera.

Lemass's reply makes interesting reading for it gives not only his personal view on how the repeal of the External Relations Act

Seán Lemass (left) and his brother Noel (courtesy Mr and Mrs John O' Connor)

J. T. LEMASS,
HATTER AND OUTFITTER,
2 and 3 Capel Street, Dublin
IRISH-MADE GOODS A SPECIALITY.

Advertisement for the Lemass family business in 'Nationality', 1917 (private collection)

Frances Lemass, Seán Lemass's mother (courtesy Mr and Mrs John O' Connor)

Junior and Middle Grade Exhibitioners, O'Connell Schools, 1915. Lemass third row, extreme left (courtesy Mr and Mrs John O'Connor)

In his father's shop, Capel Street Dublin (courtesy Mr and Mrs John O' Connor)

Photograph taken just before Seán Lemass's marriage to Kathleen Hughes
(courtesy Mr and Mrs John O' Connor)

Noel Lemass (courtesy Mr and Mrs John O' Connor)

*Lemass's Sinn Féin
membership card
(courtesy Mr and Mrs
John O' Connor)*

*Delegate card to Dublin Brigade Convention 1922
(courtesy Mr and Mrs John O' Connor)*

*Pass to Four Courts signed by
Lemass as Barrack Adjutant,
Civil War 1922
(courtesy Mr and Mrs
John O' Connor)*

*Lemass as internee at
Ballykinlar Camp
(courtesy Mr and Mrs
John O' Connor)*

Kathleen Lemass (courtesy Mr and Mrs John O' Connor)

Lemass leaving Dáil Éireann after refusing to take Oath of Allegiance
(private collection)

Fianna Party after entering Dáil Éireann, August 1927 (private collection)

On the election trail, 1932 (private collection)

Arriving at the Imperial Economic Conference, Ottawa, 1932,
with Dr James Ryan
(courtesy Mr and Mrs John O' Connor)

At the Imperial Economic Conference, 1932 with Seán T. O' Kelly and Dr James Ryan
(courtesy Mr and Mrs John O' Connor)

Fianna Fáil Government, 1938
(courtesy Mr and Mrs John O' Connor)

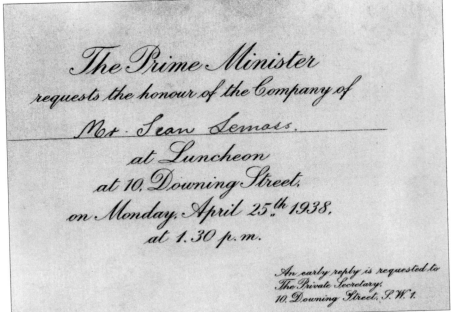

Invitation to luncheon at 10 Downing Street, 1938 (courtesy Mr and Mrs John O' Connor)

The Minister for Industry and Commerce in his Kildare Street Office
(private collection)

Relaxing at the races, 1940s (courtesy Mr and Mrs John O' Connor)

Seán and Kathleen Lemass at the RDS, 1940s (courtesy Mr and Mrs John O' Connor)

*Early days of Irish Aviation, one of Lemass's favourite projects
(courtesy Mr and Mrs John O' Connor)*

Seán Lemass with daughters Peggy and Maureen boarding Aer Lingus inaugural flight, Dublin/Paris, 1946 (private collection)

In the Vatican, 1947 (courtesy Mr and Mrs John O' Connor)

At the RDS (courtesy Mr and Mrs John O' Connor)

The 'Irish Press' gets new printing presses, 1950
(private collection)

Wedding of daughter Maureen to Charles Haughey (courtesy Mr and Mrs John O' Connor)

The extended family, photographed for 'Time', 1963 (Mr and Mrs John O' Connor)

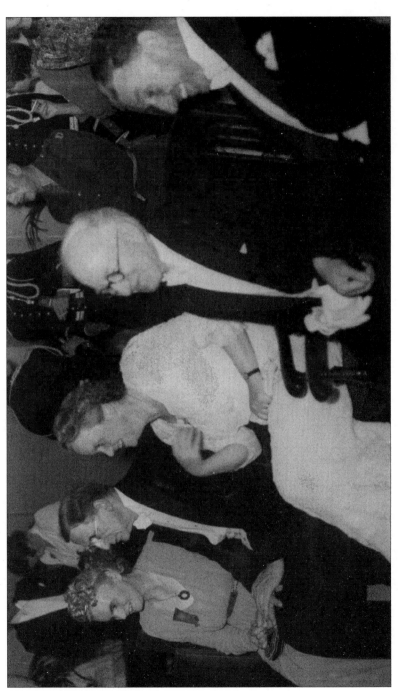

An evening at Dublin Castle. L to R Mrs Lemass, Eamon de Valera, Mrs O' Kelly, President Seán T. O' Kelly and Seán Lemass
(private collection)

Relaxing in Rome with Mrs Lemass (courtesy Mr and Mrs John O' Connor)

The Minister speaks (private collection)

The Government, 1959 (private collection)

*Kathleen Lemass at home, 1959
(private collection)*

*At the White House with John F.
Kennedy, 1963 (private collection)*

The historic meeting between Seán Lemass and Northern Ireland Prime Minister,
Captain Terence O'Neill, 1965 (private collection)

Captain O'Neill, Mrs Lemass, Mrs O'Neill and Seán Lemass on
Captain O'Neill's visit to Dublin, 1965 (private collection)

At Number 10 Downing Street with British Prime Minister, Harold Wilson, Charles Haughey and Jack Lynch, 1965 (private collection)

The Taoiseach at the Berlin Wall (private collection)

Seán Lemass and Duncan Sandys, British Colonial Secretary (private collection)

Lemass greeted by his wife at Dublin Airport. Also in picture, Eamon de Valera and Seán MacEntee (private collection)

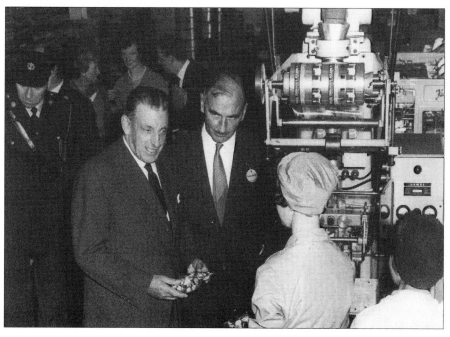

At the opening of the Urney factory with director, Redmond Gallagher (private collection)

Fishing with Brian Lenihan, 1964 (private collection)

At CIE workshop, Inchicore, 1964 (private collection)

At opening of new American Embassy, Dublin, 1964 (private collection)

At Elysée Palace, Paris, 1965, with General Charles de Gaulle and Georges Pompidou
(private collection)

Speaking at National Press Club, Washington (private collection)

With Mrs Lemass, arriving at Pro-Cathedral, Dublin, June 1963
for Requiem Mass for Pope John XXIII (private collection)

The Taoiseach in his office, 1965 (private collection)

Leaving Dublin airport for Rome, 1965 (private collection)

At Leinster House, 1965 (private collection)

Addressing Comh-Chomhairle Átha Cliath, 1966 (private collection)

With the flag which flew over GPO in 1916. Taoiseach's office, 1966
(private collection)

Arriving at his office in his last month as Taoiseach, 1966 (private collection)

In retirement, fishing in the west of Ireland, 1967 (private collection)

Maureen and Charles Haughey at the funeral of Seán Lemass, 1971

The funeral procession to Dean's Grange cemetery

unfolded but also his opinion of the relationship between the principal *dramatis personae* of the Coalition:

> Whatever opinions were held in our Party regarding the repeal of the External Relations Act – and there was more than one – it was our general view that when it was proposed by the Government there was no alternative to supporting it. In doing so, however, we made clear our view that there could be no retracting of steps along that road. Personally I should be surprised to learn that our present Government had any clear idea of where they were going in this matter. Even the suggestion of an intrigue suggests some forethought which I honestly do not believe was given. No doubt – when it was too late they tried to check its consequences, but soley to avoid an adverse political reaction here.

He went on to tell Harrison that he believed the Coalition was unlikely to work out a consistent policy and apply it intelligently and he finished off his letter with his opinion of the Taoiseach and the Minister for External Affairs:

> I think Mr MacBride is a real disaster and Costello has so little understanding of the issues that Mr MacBride's influence is supreme. I think that it would only make matters worse to encourage any attempt at a solution until we get rid of them.

The majority of Lemass's replies to Captain Harrison were courteous but guarded. With each letter from the Captain there came a new conspiracy theory, including one suggesting that MacBride (himself no stranger to the conspiracy theory) had agents at work against the Anti-Partition League. Copies of several telegrams to Harrison from Lemass show that he resisted all invitations to address League meetings in London, though both he and de Valera sent the standard form of 'good wishes' telegram to such gatherings. The correspondence ends when Fianna Fáil was returned to office in 1951.

Though not one of the most inspired periods of his career, these years out of government saw Lemass channel his energies in some new directions and renew some old ideas.

He returned to his old pursuit of looking at how best the party might be organised to come back from electoral defeat. Disappointed with the lack of will he found amongst his colleagues to analyse the reasons why they lost office in '48, Lemass buried himself in the task of organising effective parliamentary opposition, often stepping in for de Valera, and not only when de Valera went off on a world tour in which he preached on the evils of partition. He spoke on the vote for the Taoiseach's departmental estimate, as well as replying to the Budget speech in 1948 and 1949 and continued to harangue Dan Morrissey on matters relating to Industry and Commerce.

He told Michael Mills of the risk the party faced when out of government:

> As far as Fianna Fáil was concerned, there was a risk which we fully recognised that the great organisation which we had built up throughout the country would begin to disintegrate when it found the party for the first time in opposition. So we embarked on a very vigorous re-organisation campaign in which the members of the previous government were free to participate; so that by 1951 we had a much more effective organisation than we had in 1948.
>
> It was during this period in opposition that he was appointed Managing Director of the *Irish Press* Group. The job was no sinecure and Lemass became a familiar figure in the Burgh Quay offices, contributing not just to the administration but to the newspaper itself. He was closely involved in the establishment of the *Sunday Press* and before the title was launched went to London to study newspaper production methods there. He also took up a number of directorships at this time which helped make up the loss of a minister's salary and expenses.

He recovered that loss when the Coalition fell from power in May 1951 over what is usually described as a battle between Church and State but was in reality a broader issue which had as much to do with internal Coalition conflict as it had to do with conflict between Crozier and Dáil.

The coalition's troubles began when Dr Noel Browne, sought to reactivate and expand part of a legislative initiative which originated with his predecessor Dr Jim Ryan. Essentially the so-called Mother and Child Scheme proposed giving a free health service to pregnant mothers and post-natal care for mothers and for children up to the age of 16. The scheme was to be operated without a means test. The details of the objections which followed from the Roman Catholic hierarchy and the medical profession after Dr Browne's announcement of the scheme are complex and are now familiar territory. Most observers agree that Dr Browne handled the affair in a way which showed considerable lack of political instinct. Most historians and commentators who have written on the débâcle agree that there have been few such occasions in the history of the modern Irish state when a minister has been so thoroughly and shamelessly deserted by his party leader and his cabinet colleagues. De Valera assumed a stony silence during the Dáil debate on Browne's dismissal. 'We have heard enough' was the Fianna Fáil leader's only contribution to the debate. His silence, Dr Browne said, meant that he and his party 'joined the political pygmies on the government benches'.

Lemass told Michael Mills in 1969 he felt the Mother and Child Scheme was a God-given gift to Costello and MacBride in the form of an opportunity to shaft Noel Browne, who by 1951 had become an uncomfortable thorn in the Coalition's side. It was also a God-given gift to Fianna Fáil. At the age of 69 de Valera led the 'soldiers of destiny' into another electoral battle.

With Clann na Poblachta's credibility damaged by the Mother and Child Scheme and by its performance in coalition, it suffered heavy losses in the election, losing eight seats. Some of that lost support reverted to Fianna Fáil but it only gained one seat. Fine Gael gained 9. Labour and National Labour had kissed and made up in 1950 but lost 3 seats. Noel Browne and two other deputies who supported him were returned as Independents. The state of the parties was:

Fianna Fáil	69
Fine Gael	40
Labour	16
C. na Poblachata	2
C. na Talmhan	6
Independents	14

Fianna Fáil was five seats short of forming a government. On 4 June Lemass described for Henry Harrison in London, the situation in which the party found itself:

> The Election result was indecisive, and what may happen on June 13 when the Dáil meets is still a very open matter. Fianna Fáil has five seats more than the other parties, but there are fourteen 'independent' *[sic]* deputies. Of these, five are indistinguishable from Fine Gael members, so really the position is that the remaining nine have the fate of the country in their hands. The position cannot be satisfactory no matter what happens, but the only prospect of some effective work being done is if Fianna Fáil can succeed in forming a government. Another Coalition, dependent on the support of nearly all these Independent deputies offers a very depressing prospect.

Such a prospect did not materialise. With the support of those very Independents which Lemass was concerned about, and also with the support of Noel Browne (who later joined Fianna Fáil) the party was back in power and Lemass returned to the helm of Industry and Commerce.

10

RETURN TO KILDARE STREET

The situation which Fianna Fáil inherited in 1951 was most inauspicious. The balance of payments deficit stood at £62,000,000. Emigration was at its highest since the 1880s. There was an air about of general discontent with the unemployment problem, sluggish growth and the halting by the US of Marshall Aid, coupled with America's demand for early repayment of its loans.

These ills could not be laid at the door of the departing Coalition. If it had remained in office for another year it would be easier to assess its economic record but with so many external influences such an assessment is difficult. Lemass returned to his desk at Industry and Commerce in Kildare Street, in this unhappy climate.

He faced other problems as well as the economic. De Valera, whose eyesight had been deteriorating since 1936, was admitted to a hospital in Utrecht, thus leaving Lemass, as Tánaiste, with additional burdens. They included some major, and at times thorny legislative matters which de Valera directed, as it were, by remote control from his hospital bed in Utrecht where his secretary, Kathleen O'Connell, took dictation from the blinded Taoiseach.

In his new government de Valera reappointed Dr Jim Ryan as Minister for Health and Social Welfare, and it fell to him to reactivate the legislation which had been the undoing of Noel Browne and on which the Fianna Fáil leader had remained silent. De Valera quite naturally wished to avoid confrontation with the hierarchy but despite the fact that he knelt regularly to kiss the episcopal ring, and was a loyal son of the Church, he did not have Costello's penchant for grovelling before the sight of a mitred prelate. The bottom line was that de Valera was a far shrewder political animal, especially when it came to dealing with the hierarchy, than either Costello or Browne. A series of tactical concessions were made to the Health Act, including the introduction of a modest means test, and the Hierarchy and the truculent Irish Medical Association were defused. The decision to reintroduce the legislation may also have been a sop to Noel Browne who was now voting with the government.

Lemass was very much involved in the reintroduction of the health legislation, as letters to him from de Valera reveal.

In a letter of 3 November 1952, de Valera warned Lemass of the inherent dangers of the health legislation. He said that for years he had 'been afraid of the Health Service, not because of the ecclesiastical implications, but because of the difficulty in getting a workable rather than a comprehensive scheme'. He advised Lemass that Dr Ryan should be able to 'find out what are the snags which must be avoided' when dealing with the Church. De Valera's letter continues:

> I am so much afraid of the difficulties in getting a *workable* [de Valera's emphasis] scheme in regard to the Mother and Child Service that if I were at home I would urge that we first concentrate on that side of the question – making sure that what we propose can really be carried out.

De Valera said he felt that relying on an appeal to the hierarchy, in the light of what happened to Noel Browne's proposals, would be 'a terrible mistake'.

> Such an appeal might have succeeded on the former occasion when the matter arose originally, but I have very little hope that it would succeed now. The last state would be worst than the first. We must not risk that.

De Valera's caution, which so often annoyed Lemass, was evident in the letter, when he continued:

> Dr Ryan knows the practical medical side and the existing position sufficiently well to know what is feasible. If the ideal which he has in mind cannot be achieved now, but rather at

a later stage, we should definitely say so, and deliberately confine ourselves to what can immediately be done. We can indicate that what we propose are steps on the way to the ultimate goal if that be deemed desirable.

Mindful of what happened to Noel Browne after his meeting with the Church authorities and as if to stress his worries of his government's dealings with the hierarchy in his absence, de Valera returned to the subject in a postscript to the letter:

> To avoid misunderstanding later, any agreements which Dr Ryan arrives at in conversations with the ecclesiastical authorities should be reduced to writing on the spot and the terms agreed upon by both sides. He can ask for this because it is clearly necessary that there should be no possibility of misunderstanding as to what was actually agreed to. He should also agree that the terms are unambiguous.

Lemass clearly had his instructions – de Valera was not about to allow a repeat of the Mother and Child Scheme débâcle under his stewardship.

The health legislation still concerned de Valera when he wrote to Lemass six days later. In a classic example of de Valera double-speak the Chief told Lemass that if the hierarchy wanted to know his (de Valera's) position, Lemass was to say he was too ill to consider the matter in 'the detailed consideration which it would require'. He then went on to give the matter the most detailed consideration. Lemass was instructed as follows:

> ...every member of the Government should first acquaint himself with the traditional position taken up by the Church in Church versus State disputes. The best place to find that for present purposes is in a statement made by the Archbishop of Cashel at Rockwell College some time ago... The next fundamental document is that sent by Bishop Staunton in 1947. If this be carefully studied, it will be seen that it was the 'unlimited', 'unqualified', and 'absolute' powers of the Minister taken in the Act which were objected to.

De Valera told Lemass that those objections could be met by inserting the necessary qualifications and safeguards in a manner similar to those adopted in the Constitution. He also said Archbishop McQuaid's point by point objections should be gone through and he should be asked to make a draft with the qualifications which would satisfy him. That draft could then be examined from 'our point of view' until an agreed text was arrived at. 'That', de Valera concluded, 'was more or less what happened in the corresponding articles in the Constitution'.

Dr Noel Browne had been critical of de Valera for the way in which he appeared to wash his hands of the Mother and Child debate, and it seems a fair criticism from de Valera's silence at that time, but if what de Valera wrote to Lemass is correct, it appears he did not know as much as it was thought he did when the affair first exploded:

> The point is to reconcile the rights of the individual with the rights of the community. As far as I am concerned I am not able to help as I would like, because I do not know what transpired in the discussions between the Bishops and the Minister for Health, and later with the Tánaiste.

Part of the problem with Dr Browne's approach when he tried to implement the Mother and Child Scheme was that it did not have full and detailed consideration from the Coalition partners, and did not have the backing of all the cabinet. De Valera cautioned Lemass that the health legislation should be fully discussed and 'carefully considered' by 'all Ministers and the Government as a whole'. Lemass was party to the negotiations with the Catholic hierarchy and met Archbishop McQuaid, Bishop Browne of Galway, Bishop Lucey of Cork and Bishop Staunton of Ferns in December together with Dr Ryan. There were still objections from the hierarchy at that stage, but de Valera on his return from Utrecht, used the offices of the Irish Ambassador to the Vatican, Joseph Walshe, to secure theological opinion in Rome which did not support the Irish bishops' stance. Armed with this information the government was able to get the health legislation through the Oireachtas just three days before the 1954 general election.

This Utrecht correspondence is important. These letters show clearly not only how de Valera had begun to rely on his Tánaiste but how difficult and indecisive he could still be on major and minor matters. This side of de Valera's character infuriated Lemass, especially on economic decisions. De Valera has often been accused of presiding over a clerical republic and there is some justification for the charge. The Utrecht letters however show that de Valera was not prepared to have his ministers bullied by the bishops on the health legislation. His resolve was not as firm on other matters and his record in relation to episcopal pressure for censorship of 'evil publications' is appalling. In 1954 the Irish reading public was 'protected' from certain works of Christopher Isherwood, Noel Coward, John Steinbeck, Jean-Paul Sartre, Frank O'Connor and Seán O'Casey.

On 27 September 1952 de Valera informed Lemass that he would have to represent him during the Budget debate and on the Estimates for the Taoiseach's Department, if he felt sufficiently unwell to be present himself. He told him he could deal with the task 'in your own way'. 'Mr Lemass is capable of explaining government policy with a clarity, authority, and breadth of vision far beyond the reach of any of his colleagues', the *Leader* wrote in a budget preview. 'When Mr MacEntee presents a statement of the same policy', the article continued, 'it seems to have become incoherent, distorted, and attenuated.'

The 1952 Budget was considered a 'bombshell' of the most stinging variety. MacEntee, back in Finance, much to Lemass's annoyance, delivered it and in doing so raised income tax by a shilling in the pound, and with it, raised the price of tea, bread, butter, milk, sugar, petrol, and alcohol.

'Difficult, almost to the verge of desperation' is how MacEntee described the country's finances in late January 1952. His department defended the harsh budget by reference to the appalling balance of payments situation. Such an explanation was cold comfort to a population feeling the pinch of the miserable 1950s. The Labour Party called a protest rally in Dublin after which there were disturbances in which several people were injured. However, the irony was that MacEntee's budget was a qualified success; the external trading account looked healthier a year later, domestic consumption was down and the demanded for imports had also been reduced. But as Joseph Lee points out, while MacEntee's policy was honest and courageous, its 'identification with austerity helped to condemn the government to premature demise, when Independent deputies withdrew their support in May 1954'. That hard political reality also stymied any ambition MacEntee had of succeeding de Valera, thus leaving the way clear for Lemass to inherit the leadership of Fianna Fáil. There was, at least, one area of agreement between Lemass and MacEntee, and that was consensus on the matter that Irish external assets should not be wasted on the importation of goods for consumption on the domestic market. There the agreement ended; otherwise in this period Lemass was marginalised at cabinet by MacEntee's dominance as Minister for Finance. Lemass was also troubled by health problems. He underwent surgery for gall-bladder complaints and his health became a matter for public comment and concerns about it were reported in the *Irish Press*.

If his pre-eminence at the cabinet table was eclipsed by MacEntee, it did not prevent him ploughing ahead with fresh initiatives within his own ministerial ambit. Three such initiatives dominated these years; he encouraged the view that the investment of foreign capital would be of considerable benefit to the economy, he began a critical review of restrictive practices and protectionism and he encouraged an expansionist programme which involved attempting to persuade the banks into playing a greater role in the development of the economy.

The investment of foreign capital was an emotive issue. Its promotion ended the republican dream of self-sufficiency and it was therefore an issue that had to be handled sensitively. 'We welcome foreign capital coming into Irish industrial development when it brings with it new opportunities for expansion and new industrial techniques', Lemass declared cautiously on May Day 1953. Lemass had been thinking about foreign investment since at least 1948. Now he said the stable political situation in Ireland was the basis for security in investment. The time for imposing restrictions on foreign investment in Ireland had long since past. To prove his point he told American businessmen in New York on 8 October 1953 : 'The payment of interest and dividends on external investment is freely permitted and capital gains may also be repatriated'.

The *New York Herald Tribune* reported Lemass telling the Commerce and Industry Association in New York that Ireland planned a three-pronged programme of investments, an expanded tourist trade, and increased exports. He said a special dollar marketing group had been set up to direct the programme. He told his audience that the Irish economy in the past had been financed domestically but the government had come round to the view that the time had come 'when a limited investment of external capital is desirable'. He said such capital investment would be welcome 'provided it is directed to projects that increased Irish productive capacity' or brought in new techniques. A double-taxation agreement protected American investors from an undue tax burden. In New York, Lemass opened the first US office of Córas Tráchtála (one had just been opened in Montreal).

Yet a note of caution sounded in Lemass when he spoke of 'limited investment of foreign capital'. It was just as well that he showed some restraint as he was soon coming under attack, though mostly from the lunatic fringe of economic nationalism. The President of NAIDA, Patrick Moylett, lambasted Lemass for his view on foreign capital. He told his members on 5 June exactly what he thought of Mr Lemass's heresy:

From 1932 to the end of March last the policy of the various governments was to secure the control of Irish industries to Irish nationals. On May 1st last Mr Lemass issued an invitation to foreigners to come in and invest in Ireland....There are about 800 alien institutions operating in this country squeezing the life-blood out of our shopkeepers who financed the Land League, Sinn Féin and Republican movements. This thing could not happen in France, Italy or South Africa. But in a statement on May 1st Sean Lemass is inviting foreigners now to help....This is cutting across all our national work. It has made us so depressed we cannot hold our heads up.

The criticism did not end there. Lemass's old sparring partner P.W. Murphy of the Federation of Irish Manufacturers accused Lemass of creating 'a climate of uncertainty'. Other manufacturers expressed public concern about the fate of their protective tariffs. Lemass, as an astute observer of the relationship of big business to party political support, must have been mindful how Fianna Fáil's share of that bounty had been threatened by his policies in 1947. If he had forgotten it, and that is most unlikely, Fine Gael would have reminded him of it, as they had quite successfully attempted to take business support away from Fianna Fáil, in the run-up to the '48 election. The irate merchant princes were not the only citizens worried about the withdrawal of protection. Workers in some industries feared that their jobs were on the line. In the face of such opposition, Lemass had little option but to retreat, restrained again by the political realities until the time was right to make a decisive strike.

He summed up Ireland's industrial situation, as he saw it, when he spoke in Boston in October '53:

Industry in Ireland, which is still a 50 percent agricultural country, is constantly increasing and developing. But one of our chief problems is still emigration, and this problem cannot be eliminated or reduced to a normal rate unless we get a greater variety of trades at home. To continue to develop we must find a wider export market for our products.

The support of state expenditure in the widest possible sense became part of the Lemass canon. He had advanced considerably in the belief that Ireland's external assets could be used for purposes other than to support export-oriented productive capital. On 11 November 1953 the *Irish Press* reported him thus:

There was no sense in keeping abroad financial reserves which might be more profitable employed at home. He did not confine their use to profitable in the financial sense. He disagreed with the implication in the Central Bank report that there should only be repatriation of assets if they earned more at home than they earned abroad. They should be satisfied if the general social consequence was sufficient to justify the change.

Economists, amongst them Professor George O'Brien, the grand old man of Irish economics, supported the Central Bank's view. But the banking system was being criticised for failing to make credit available to industry. The criticism came not just from the popular press but from the conservative *Irish Times* and elements within Fine Gael. Lemass, however, did not confront the banks head-on, rather he favoured the development of a new policy line as the preferred route. By 1954 that included requesting the IDA to take a fresh and critical look at the whole policy of protection.

The minority government of 1951-54 was as ineffectual as its inter-party predecessor in coming to grips with the chronically depressed Irish economy of the period. It was Lemass's dullest and least innovative period in office. He looked back at the period himself in this light and while he was critical of his colleagues for their conservatism, it must be said that he too seemed to opt for the safe approach of financial stability rather than policy innovation at that time. There were some legislative developments, many of them engaged to counter decisions taken by the previous administration. The transatlantic air service was given fresh support; the ESB was encouraged to develop the use of turf in electricity generation; the export board, Córas Tráchtála, came on stream; the fisheries board, Bórd Iascaigh Mhara, was established in 1952; the Underdeveloped Areas Bill – a measure aimed at developing rural Ireland by grant-aiding the establishment of industry in the west and south-west – was vigorously defended by Lemass against opposition charges of political chicanery by Fianna Fáil. Lemass was accused by the opposition of using the measure to bolster Fianna Fáil's falling support in those regions.

Encouraged by similar legislation in Britain, Lemass introduced the Restrictive Trade Practices Bill, in the hope of undoing some of the damage done by three comforting decades of protection. His efforts were denounced by the Chamber of Commerce as 'drastic' and unnecessary. Several trade associations who were cosseted by the umbrella of protection also denounced the measure, but Lemass got the bill successfully through the Dáil.

The government survived a confidence vote in July 1953 but its parliamentary position was weak and getting weaker, as signs of social unrest began to show on the streets. The unemployed organised marches which sometimes turned into confrontation with the Gárdaí. Members of the Dublin Unemployed Association were imprisoned after clashes in the capital. A concerned de Valera circulated a memorandum to his ministers proposing that employment be stimulated as a matter of priority. Lemass's department responded with an overview of its achievement on the employment and industrial development fronts. The department estimated that 46,000 jobs had been created between 1951 and 1953 through the expenditure of £23,000,000 of public funds. It also estimated that between April 1951 and February 1953, nearly 150 new industries had been established while proposals for 200 more were under consideration by Lemass and his staff.

Lemass met trade union leaders and the Labour Party in July 1953 to discuss the unemployment crisis in the construction industry. Between 1951 and 1955 the sector lost over 6,000 jobs. It was put to Lemass that the country was facing a depression but he rejected that view, supporting his argument with the evidence of an increase in both national income and personal consumption. Soon after that meeting he advocated an increase in state spending to stimulate the economy. It was clear to Lemass that the level of private investment was insufficient to induce the sort of expansion he envisaged and he stated this in a memorandum of 28 July 1953:

> Many forms of production are now at the limits of existing market needs. Increased export possibilities, so far as manufacturing industry is concerned, are not substantial enough to produce investment on an adequate scale. Only a rising population, with rising living standards, will create a situation in which the expansion of industrial and commercial activity will involve a regular expansion of private capital investment to a degree that will encourage normal employment.

MacEntee rejected Lemass's view that enough growth could be generated in the economy to absorb the mass of the unemployed. This position of MacEntee's supports the contention that the Minister for Finance did not accept the view that Irish industry was likely to supplant the dominance of agriculture at that time. Lemass was openly critical of farming methods and expressed reservations about the way the farm subsidy system worked. A profile in *The Irish Times* in July 1953 pointed to Lemass's urban bias : 'Fianna Fáil is primarily the party of the small farmer. Mr Lemass is essentially a townsman...whether he could exert a national influence is doubtful'. *The Irish Times* went even further and suggested that he might well be leaving politics for a job in private industry. This was the first time that public comment suggested that Lemass might not succeed de Valera as leader of Fianna Fáil. Yet we find the *Boston Globe* in October 1953 writing of him as 'a possible successor to Eamon de Valera'.

As already noted the dissatisfaction of the unemployed manifested itself in street unrest, and it gave the government cause for serious concern by early 1954. There was also the litmus test of by-elections to contend with. Out of three by-elections held in June 1952, Fianna Fáil took two seats in Mayo North and in Waterford. Fine Gael took a seat in Limerick East. There were two by-elections in June 1953, in which Fine Gael took a seat from Fianna Fáil in Wicklow and from Labour in Cork East. Fianna Fáil took a seat in Galway South in August 1953. But on 4 March 1954, when de Valera heard of Fianna Fáil by-elections defeats in Louth and in Cork City, he called a general election. Lemass was appointed national director of elections.

The campaign which he ran was not particularly distinguished. He engaged in the old rhetoric of Fine Gael bashing, instilling in the electorate the fear that Fine Gael was anti-industrial in outlook, and if returned to power 'could do real damage to the country's prospects'.

Lemass told the electorate it was a very easy matter to establish what the opposition was against, but it was considerably more difficult to establish what they were for. The election debate never got around to a consideration of the real issues of economic policy. Fianna Fáil campaigned on its record and that record, in May 1954, smacked of economic conservatism.

Fianna Fáil hoped to make gains in those rural areas, where *The Irish Times* considered Lemass's writ ineffective. An increase of two seats would have given it an overall majority. Lemass knew then, others in the party would know later, that it was the urban vote that needed to be wooed.

Nearly 1,500,000 people turned out to vote. Fianna Fáil won 65 seats leaving it 10 short of an overall majority. Fine Gael won 50 and Labour made 4 gains, giving it 19 seats. Clann na Poblachta took 3 and Clann na Talmhan 5 seats; the Independents also won 5 seats.

Lemass's personal vote had been dropping since 1948 when, in Dublin South Central, he won 13,275 first preferences. In 1951 it dropped to 10,759; and in 1954 to 7,753. In Lemass's constituency in '51, Fianna Fáil gained a seat from Clann na Poblachta's Con Lehane (a solicitor who defended IRA activists) and in 1954 Fianna Fáil's Philip Brady lost a seat to Fine Gael's T.A. Finlay.

John A. Costello returned to power with the support of Labour and Clann na Talmhan. William Norton became Tánaiste and assumed Lemass's portfolio at Industry and Commerce. Lemass returned to the role he had so readily taken to in the late 1920s, that of Fianna Fáil national organiser.

11

Waiting in the Wings

The backward looking fifties, were, as the author Bernard Share has dubbed them 'something of a splendid anachronism'. 'Modernisation proceeded piecemeal and by stealth,' Mr Share writes of a decade in which the reality of mass emigration left no area of the country untouched. 'Motor car registration marks, established under the British regime at the dawn of the automobile era, were still barely into three letter combinations...the telephone number of the Imperial Hotel, Castlebar, was still Castlebar 3, and, one of the attractions of its twenty-five bedrooms was, an advertisement assured the public, "electric light". It was still possible to travel by train from Thurles to Clonmel via Horse and Jockey, from Roscrea to Birr, from Kilfree Junction to James Dillon's Ballaghadereen and by the unique West Clare, from Ennis to Craggagknock, Shragh, Moyasta Junction and Kilkee...'

Gerard Sweetman, a solicitor, became Minister for Finance in Costello's new administration and with William Norton at Industry and Commerce presided over a most troubled period for the Irish economy. In 1954 the balance of payments deficit was £5.5 million, by 1955 it had risen to £35.6 million, thus reducing the country's external reserves to a level inadequate for any emergencies that might arise. Sweetman imposed new taxes on consumer goods and imposed import levies on a large range of goods. The Coalition was engaged in the introduction of drastic measures to save what Sweetman called 'our economic independence'. The Minister for Finance's position was unenviable; his policies lacked the support of his Taoiseach and Tánaiste, who in turn were under pressure from the trade union movement, which was actively critical of the Coalition government. The unions were especially annoyed about the cut-backs on public services, especially housing.

Costello's administration fought, with great difficulty, to halt the unions' increasing militancy, and in the hope of diffusing the situation, announced a new national development plan in October 1956. What made the plan interesting was its emphasis on foreign capital, a notion Lemass had supported three years earlier, but now, suddenly, seemed to have gone lukewarm on.

Norton went on a European and American tour drumming up support from foreign investors. The first to bite was an oil conglomerate which invested £12,000,000 in an oil refinery in Cork harbour. It all had a striking resemblence to the sort of policy initiative Lemass had supported for some years but his reaction to it was quite surprising. He had called for foreign investment and he had supported the establishment of an oil refinery, though in Dublin. Even the tone of Norton's public statements could quite easily be taken for Lemass-speak:

> The whole purpose of stimulating external investment in Irish industry is to promote the establishment of new types of industries and to secure an expansion that would not otherwise take place. Irish manufacturers who are catering efficiently for the needs of the market may, therefore, rest assured that their interests will be fully safeguarded.

The usual conservative sources criticised Norton's initiative. He was accused of 'selling out' Ireland's native manufacturers for the lure of foreign capital. Costello felt the need to intervene and he reassured Irish industrialists that his minister meant that foreign capital would only be welcome for 'the production of goods not already produced here' or for 'the production of goods for export'.

In opposition Fianna Fáil was vehemently opposed to allowing an open-door policy for foreign investors. De Valera spoke of 'keeping Ireland for the Irish' and Kevin Boland was also worried that foreign capital would have a serious effect on national independence. Erskine Childers also expressed doubts. But the greatest ambiguity surrounded Lemass's own stance. He had openly supported the notion in 1953, with limited reservation, and would do so again in government, but he baulked at Norton's proposals and withdrew to beat the drum of economic nationalism.

His reaction to Norton's foreign investment scheme had echoes of his position on the matter in 1929 when he said:

> Their [foreign investors] only interest in the country is the profit they can make out of it...Secondly, industries which are only branches of foreign concerns...seldom develop an export trade. It is usual also for the higher executives...to be employees...from the parent branch.

Bew and Patterson, who have analysed Lemass's ambiguity on the issue of foreign investment in great detail, observe it as 'part of the retreat back to economic nationalism [which] gave the Fianna Fáil leadership a semblance of unity. Loyalty to a shared vision of the past was substituted for an agreed common programme for the present. It was a shoddy and unimpressive device', the authors claim.

If it suited his purposes Lemass had no difficulty in paying reverent lip-service to de Valera's vision of bucolic bliss or, as Charles Haughey put it, 'He had no objection to the idea of comely maidens dancing at the crossroads but he preferred to see them working in factories.'

It seems particularly odd that Lemass should have engaged in such economic nationalism, just a year after he made what became known as the 100,000 jobs or Clery's restaurant speech of 16 October 1955. The speech, based not entirely on original thinking, but partly on a variant of a plan presented in Italy, was a prelude to the much lauded Whitaker Plan. The speech was another example of how Lemass kept himself closely briefed on developing economic trends in Europe. It proposed an investment programme of some £67,000,000 million of government money, coupled with private investment, to create a proposed 100,000 jobs in the private sector within five years.

The first 'Irish Keynesian proclamation' Erskine Childers called the speech. 'A simple Keynesian prescription of increased public investment to generate 100,000 new jobs' Dr Kenneth Whitaker called it. T.K. Whitaker had been appointed as Secretary of the Department of Finance by Sweetman, and with economists like Patrick Lynch, represented the new breed of thinkers who greatly influenced the direction of public policy in the 1950s and beyond. Whitaker's paper, *Economic Development*, now venerated as one of the great classics of Irish economic writing, had a profound effect on the way politicians thought about the economy. Nevertheless one cabinet minister who served under Lemass is of the opinion that the 'build-up of Whitaker as architect of modern economic planning fitted in neatly with latent media hostility to Fianna Fáil and a refusal to give Lemass credit for his own achievements'. The same former minister says Whitaker is unlikely to have advanced his proposals very far if he had been dealing with Seán MacEntee as Minister for Finance.

Lemass's speech at Clery's, though flawed for setting too optimistic an employment target, did have the effect of stimulating a more wide-ranging economic debate and prompted Costello to produce his 1956 plan, mentioned above. Apart from its emphasis on foreign capital, the Costello plan placed even greater emphasis on agricultural research and tax incentives for exports. Fianna Fáil dismissed it as yet another Coalition 'plan for tomorrow', Fine Gael had already dismissed Lemass's speech at Clery's as an attempt to bribe the electorate with job promises. Though in reality Lemass's speech was, as Sweetman described it in the Dáil, 'semi-Keynesian', it was also a serious attempt on his part to bring Fianna Fáil around to the principle of planning. Sweetman hit a nerve when he accused Fianna Fáil of lacking unity when it came to which financial policy they wished to put before the people. Sweetman was correct when he pointed out that Aiken and MacEntee did not accept Lemass's Keynesian approach, as indeed was Costello when he made the same point on a few occasions before the 1957 general election. Without party unity Lemass's approach could have little hope of success no matter what the nature of the language in which he dressed his plans. In January 1957 he laid the groundwork for the abandonment of many of the sacred cows of Fianna Fáil orthodoxy but his plans were couched in the sort of language that would not upset the party conservatives.

Without the pressure of ministerial work to attend to, Lemass was involved with plans other than the economic. He once told Charles Haughey he believed 'the hardest thing to do in politics was to keep a party togther in opposition'. As Fianna Fáil National Organiser he withdrew to the backrooms of Fianna Fáil GHQ, where with a new generation of 'young Turks' he planned not just how to keep the party unified in opposition but how best to move it on the return road to power. His daughters recall this period as one of the happier times in his life. He enjoyed the company of the younger men who were anxious to put their stamp on the party. They included his son-in-law Charles Haughey, Brian Lenihan, Kevin Boland, and Eoin Ryan.

These men formed the backbone of an organisation committee which set about the task of rebuilding the Fianna Fáil organisation to fight the next general election. Lemass travelled around the country, with various members of the committee, pruning the cumainn of the old organisation of their dead wood; settling disputes; instilling pride in the organisation's workers and also instilling in them the belief that Fianna Fáil would form a single party government with a comfortable majority, next time out.

Charles Haughey remembers those days:

> We were a task force. We travelled the length and breadth of the country at weekends and sometimes during the week. We divided the country up between us covering it area by area, and visiting every cumainn, culminating in a meeting of the Comhairle Dáil Ceantair which would put our suggestions on stream. I always did a written report for Lemass and he would decide what had to be done.

Lemass once requested a party official in Tipperary to submit a written report detailing the condition of the organisation there. The offical wrote back complaining that 'organisations that exist on paper are no good to Fianna Fáil and won't win elections'. Lemass, in a return missive, informed the truculant Tipperary official that 'organisations that cannot be put on paper are no good either'.

Lemass used a body called Comh-Comhairle Átha Cliath to initiate public debate on policy matters that were of interest to him. He also used it to gain sympathy for those policies within the party. The organisation, of which Charles Haughey was secretary, organised public lectures and discussions, especially on economic matters. 'It was', Charles Haughey recalls, 'always open to new ideas and non-members of Fianna Fáil were welcome.' Lemass's speech at Clery's was made under the auspices of the Comh-Comhairle. At one meeting, which was addressed by Bishop Kavanagh of Dublin, a member of the organisation, caught in a moment of religious fervour, suggested to the bishop that Seán Lemass would lead a rosary crusade for the salvation of the country. The bishop replied that Lemass would, perhaps, be better employed continuing his economic crusade for the country's salvation.

Brian Farrell catches the mood of the man waiting in the wings for de Valera to go:

> Looking back on these years the younger men recall the reorganisation enterprise in terms of excitement, exhilaration and achievement. Lemass seemed fully to share that positive mood. He was always ready to listen to and consider their suggestions. He forged powerful bonds of shared experience with a group a generation removed from his own. If he had any regrets as he revitalised the party at the expense of the old-timers, he typically masked that emotion behind his cultivated facade of disciplined detachment. Perhaps he felt no pangs. Certainly in later years he was clearly of the opinion, though in a slightly different context, that 'there are too many people who have stayed on too long'.

As the 1957 election approached, such thoughts were exercised though never publicly articulated, in relation to the leadership of the 75 year-old de Valera. Costello sounded the death-knell of his own administration in January 1957 when he spoke of the lacklustre performance of the economy. The government's performance in countering IRA terrorism was more successful but it proved too much for veteran republican Seán MacBride who tabled a no-confidence motion in the government. Rather than face possible defeat Costello called an election for 5 March. The Coalition's majority had been reduced through the course of seven by-elections held since the general election. De Valera led Fianna Fáil into his last general election. He did so on an anti-Coalition platform with Lemass following on behind thumping home the message that the country could not tolerate a ten per cent unemployment rate. The strategy worked. Out came the protest vote and Fianna Fáil was returned to office with 78 seats, a majority of 9, which was augmented by the absence of the 4 victorious Sinn Féin candidates who did not take up their Dáil seats. Three of those seats were won at the expense of Fianna Fáil. Amongst the deputies returned was Lemass's son, Noel, and his son-in-law, Charles Haughey. Fine Gael took 40 seats and Labour 12, Clann na Talmhan 3, and 9 Independents were returned. Seán MacBride lost his seat. The election ushered in a sixteen-year period in which Fianna Fáil would dominate.

De Valera formed his last cabinet, in which Lemass again retained the Industry and Commerce portfolio and the post of Tánaiste. Also ushered in was the period in which, as Neil Blaney recalled, the party began to wonder, not so much when de Valera would go but when Lemass would take over as Taoiseach. MacEntee was not reappointed to Finance – a clear signal that his influence was on the wane and that in the leadership stakes he was not *papabile*. There is general agreement in Fianna Fáil that MacEntee was never really considered to be leadership material. It has not been possible to establish if de Valera was pressurised by Lemass to remove MacEntee from Finance. But it is quite likely that he discussed the possibility with de Valera. MacEntee was still being blamed by elements of the party for losing it the 1954 general election because of his hairshirt budgets. Nor has it been possible to establish if Lemass put pressure on de Valera to replace Gerry Boland with his son Kevin Boland who became a minister on his first day in the Dáil. Again Lemass was the person most likely to exhert such influence. Gerry Boland and Lemass had grown apart over the years and had disagreements not just on policy matters but on matters of party organisation. It has even been suggested that their differences rested simply on Boland's jealousy of Lemass. Such internal party strife gave credence to the view of one wag, that 'in the Ireland of the 1950s the biggest growth industry was begrudgery'.

There have been various accounts of the circumstances which led to Lemass succeeding de Valera. Seán MacEntee and Dr Jim Ryan are said to have organised a highly secret meeting of cabinet ministers in late 1958, at which all agreed, with the exception of Frank Aiken, that de Valera should stand for the presidency. This opinion was, allegedly, reported to him by MacEntee and Ryan. MacEntee denied that the meetings ever took place. It has also been claimed that Dr Ryan made a direct personal approach to de Valera in early 1957 and his reply was simply, if the party want it then so be it. At the 1957 Árd Fheis de Valera signalled his intention of staying on as leader, as long as the party wanted him to stay.

Charles Haughey served under de Valera in his last years. He once described for Tim Pat Coogan the attitude towards de Valera remaining on as Taoiseach at that time. He described for Coogan a National Executive meeting at which de Valera rambled on about the national aims and the restoration of the language. After the meeting Haughey recalled Oscar Traynor, one of de Valera's most loyal supporters, saying 'It won't do. It won't do. The young people need jobs.' It seems unlikely that direct pressure from the cabinet was the cause of de Valera's departure from office, though there is some evidence to suggest that Oscar Traynor did make a personal approach to him. Michael McInerney, former *Irish Times* political correspondent, remembered Lemass saying 'Dev's old magic is going. He has become the adjudicator among Ministers, no longer the initiator.' The pattern for leaving office was neatly falling into place with the imminent retirement of Seán T. O'Kelly after his second term in the presidency. It is most likely that de Valera's decision to go was primarily his own, and that it was speeded up somewhat by his awareness of the opinion abroad that it was time for him to go gracefully to the Park. The message was finally driven home by Oscar Traynor who put it to him that if he were not the party's presidential candidate they would lose the election. His reply indicated that he knew his time was up, saying simply 'I am at the disposal of the party'.

Like so much of his career, de Valera's last days in office were crammed with incident. His last parliamentary battle was fought over his attempt to abandon proportional representation in the hope of securing the hegemony of Fianna Fáil in the voting system. The parliamentary battle was a success but the people rejected the proposal in a referendum.

On the eve of de Valera's departure Noel Browne introduced a Private Members Motion in the Dáil, through which he sought to have the true nature of de Valera's financial interest in the *Irish Press* made public. The basic thrust of the motion was that de Valera's shareholding in the newspaper was inconsistent with the dignity of the office of Taoiseach. The debate was held on 12 December 1958 and the motion was lost by 71 votes to 49. There was a considerable ammount of mud slinging from Browne and a feeble defence from de Valera and from MacEntee. On a normal newsday the story would have provided banner headlines for the national press but as it happened de Valera pulled a master-stroke which kept the story hidden in the inner recesses of the newspapers.

The vote on Dr Browne's motion was held on 14 January 1959 and the Fianna Fáil Parliamentary Party met on the same day. An emotional meeting was informed of de Valera's decision to step down and seek election to the presidency. It was that news which engaged the scribes who wrote the front pages of the national newspapers the following day. It was also that news which heralded to Seán Lemass that his destiny was drawing near.

It is a generally accepted view that Lemass emerged from de Valera's shadow with full benediction and without a murmur of discontent from his parliamentary colleagues. After all de Valera had publicly named him as heir apparent during two Árd Fheis speeches in his last years in office. There were still some deputies from the conservative wing of the party who were not wholly happy with the choice of Lemass. Two deputies who were present at the meeting where Lemass replaced de Valera as leader remember dissenting voices, raised not in loud clamour but in niggling discontent. They recall Gerry Boland making a petulant bitter speech which did not directly object to Lemass taking over, but rather made it clear that, as one of them put it, 'the decision wasn't in line with his thinking'. One of the deputies also recalls Joe Kennedy from Westmeath being suspicious of Lemass's intentions in relation to the party old guard, and voiced the opinion that Lemass, as the new broom, would sweep all before him and the old guard would be the first victims. He invoked a little classical learning and addressed the new leader of Fianna Fáil in the manner in which the gladiators of ancient Rome adressed the Emperor before engaging in combat: '*Ave, Caesar, morituri te salutant*'. [Hail, Caesar, those who are about to die salute you]. His failure to provide a translation was greeted with a chorus of 'Ah Jaysus Joe, would you say it in English!'

Some country deputies favoured Jim Ryan over Lemass as de Valera's replacement, but Ryan himself, one of Lemass's most loyal supporters, was not interested. Lemass assumed the leadership without a challenge and when Oscar Traynor suggested that the new leader be given every support in his drive to implement his policies there was enthuastic support for the man who had just stepped into de Valera's shoes.

When it came to the endorsement by Dáil Éireann of his nomination as Taoiseach, on 23 June 1959, the opposition, with a few exceptions, was not generous. Oliver J. Flanagan told the House he believed 'there is no person with a more dishonest public record'. John A. Costello and James Dillon charged him with breaking his promises to the Irish people and of being untrustworthy. Richard Mulcahy said he lacked understanding of many of the problems facing the country and had no sense of their magnitude. Those who were generous in their remarks included Brendan Corish of the Labour party who said Lemass had 'not got a fair crack of the whip' and he was of the opinion that Lemass's position was like that of Anthony Eden in Britain. Paddy Lindsay of Fine Gael praised his 'personal generosity in this country and abroad'. Noel Browne who was critical of Lemass's failures in the area of social policy, praised his 'solid achievements'.

Now at the age of 60 Seán Lemass was Taoiseach and leader of Fianna Fáil. The condition of Ireland's finances was well known to him; the condition of Fianna Fáil's was about to be revealed. In early July de Valera invited Lemass to his house in Cross Avenue, Blackrock. The meeting was a sort of pep talk at which the reins of power were handed over in an informal manner. De Valera had wished to inform Lemass of the exact state of party finances but the information was not available to him in time for the meeting. On 9 July he wrote to Lemass at government buildings. On the envelope of the typed letter de Valera marked, in his own hand, 'secret and personal'.

It told Lemass that the total market value of the party's investments at 15 June 1959 was estimated at £22,259. The Trustees' deposit account had a credit balance of £7,338 15s. 2d.; the Trustees' current account had a credit balance of £21,705 17s.and 6d. the F.F. Treasurees' current account had a credit balance of £2,133 8s. 2d. De Valera explained that the balance on the current account was so high due to the likelihood of heavy demands for constituency refunds and for election expenses. He advised that when those matters were settled the greater portion of the balance be put on deposit. He told Lemass that the Deed of Trust and the Deeds of the party HQ, 13 Upper Mount Street, were lodged with the Munster and Leinster Bank at O'Connell Street.

The receipt of that letter signaled that the age of de Valera had ended, and the 'rising tide' of the era of Lemass was about to break.

De Valera found it difficult to relinquish the levers of power. He continued to advise Lemass until it came to a point where Lemass was forced, very much against his will, to remind his old Chief that he was now Taoiseach. Dr David Thornley, the Trinity acdemic and Labour Party TD, once told RTE's Foreign Editor, Andrew Sheppard, that Lemass told him he had to speak very firmly with de Valera when he felt his interference from the Park was becoming intolerable. De Valera had been 'the Chief' but Lemass was now known in the party as 'the Boss'.

12
TAOISEACH

If the 1950s was the decade which closed a chapter of despair, the 1960s was the decade which opened one of hope. 'The best of decades' is how it is nostalgically remembered. There was a sense of confidence in the country generated by the emergence from de Valera's 'dreary Eden' on 'the rising tide' which, Lemass proclaimed, would 'lift all boats'. It seemed that Ireland had been spared the curious fate which one international observer feared it might suffer. In the learned journal, *Foreign Affairs*, John Kelleher, noted that so manifold were the country's problems at the end of the 1950s that it risked disappearing from history through 'an implosion upon a central vacuity'. Professor Terence Browne, of Trinity College, who drew attention to this ominous warning in his book, *Ireland:A Social and Cultural History*, reminds us that:

> The fact that this unhappy if original fate was avoided is usually credited by historians, and those who participated in the economic revival of the early 1960s, to the adventurous policies suggested by T.K. Whitaker, ably and energetically prosecuted by the Fianna Fáil Prime Minister, Seán Lemass.

In order to prosecute the reforms he wished to put in place, the general view at the time was that Lemass needed to make serious changes when he named his first cabinet. However, he chose to err on the side of caution and opted for continuity rather than radical change. Charles Haughey says Lemass had honed Fianna Fáil into a 'coherent yet traditional machine, and he was unlikely to rupture that to make changes just for change sake. When he did make cabinet changes he made them subtly and well.'

In his first cabinet he appointed Sean MacEntee as Tánaiste and Minister for Health and Social Welfare, though it is likely that he would have preferred Jim Ryan as Tánaiste. Ryan was appointed to Finance, Frank Aiken to External Affairs, Oscar Traynor to Justice and Paddy Smith to Agriculture. Thus the senior cabinet posts all went to members of 'Dev's old team'. MacEntee, Aiken and Ryan had all been in de Valera's cabinet in 1932. Oscar Traynor was first appointed to the cabinet in 1936 and Paddy Smith had been appointed Parliamentary Secretary in 1939.

The *Irish Press* assured its readers that Lemass had opted for continuity. The new members on the team were Dr Patrick Hillery who was made Minister for Education, Michael Moran at the Gaeltacht (later Gerald Bartley was appointed to that ministry), and Michael Hilliard at Posts & Telegraphs. The other appointees had served under de Valera. Jack Lynch took Lemass's old portfolio at Industry and Commerce, Erskine Childers was appointed first to Lands and later to Posts & Telegraphs, Kevin Boland to Defence and Neil Blaney was made Minister for Local Government.

Lemass expressed his belief in continuity and the maintenance of harmony when he said: 'It is far more important to maintain good will and harmony than seek a more effective distribution of responsibility.' Charles Haughey says Lemass was of the opinion that 'the appointment of Ministers was the prerogative of the Taoiseach and did not require cabinet discussion'. Though he was glad to abrogate that prerogative in the case of the appointment of his son-in-law to be Parliamentary Secretary to the Minister for Justice, Oscar Traynor. Traynor was in poor health in 1960 and requested the assistance of a parliamentary secretary. There was considerable cabinet support for the appointment of C.J. Haughey. It cleared him of any possible suggestion that the appointment was an act of nepotism on his part. Charles Haughey remembers Lemass sending for him in May 1960 and telling him of the support within cabinet for his appointment (the supporters included Neil Blaney). He informed him that it was his duty as Taoiseach to convey the government's invitation to become a parliamentary secretary but it was his duty as his father-in-law to advise him not to take it.

Lemass opened his remarks with the phrase 'It is the opinion of the government'. Within a year and a half C.J. Haughey had been appointed to the cabinet to replace Oscar Traynor as Minister for Justice where he began a process of innovative legislative reform, which even his most ardent detractors credit as mould-breaking.

Here, we return briefly to December 1957 to look at the point where Kenneth Whitaker's panacea for national recovery was presented and to consider its implications for Lemass as Taoiseach. In December 1957 the Minister for Finance, Dr Ryan, received a memorandum written by Whitaker which suggested the need for 'an integrated programme of national development for the next five or ten years'. Dr Whitaker said he believed those years to be vital 'for the country's survival as an economic entity'.

As we have already seen, the laudatory way which history recorded Dr Whitaker's role in the introduction of the move towards economic planning and the First Programme, is not quite how it was recorded in Fianna Fáil circles. There are at least two reasons for this. It was unusual then, as indeed it would still be now, for a civil servant to attain the limelight over a major policy initiative, though it must be stressed that Dr Whitaker did not seek it out, it fell upon him unsolicited. Fianna Fáil ministers of the period felt that Dr Jim Ryan's role in drawing attention to, and stoutly supporting Whitaker's plan, has gone largely unsung. Dr Ryan's secretary, Eileen Ryan, fulminated with rage at the mention of the Whitaker Plan and often complained that if it were not for her boss's support Dr Whitaker's plan would never have come to very much. While such loyalty may be touching it is somewhat removed from the truth of the situation. Credit is due to Dr Ryan for recognising the importance of what Whitaker was saying in his paper and for ensuring that it reached the ears of the right cabinet ministers, but it fell to Lemass, as Taoiseach, to recognise the urgent need to implement what Whitaker was proposing. Both Ryan and Lemass insisted that Whitaker's name appear on the published document. Lemass's reasoning was that the plan's association with a senior civil servant would distance it from the charge of political gimmickry. When the Whitaker memorandum came up for cabinet discussion Lemass told his colleagues that what was now being proposed was what he himself had recommended. His remarks had all the hallmarks of an 'I told you so' admonishment. 'I told you all these things. I put these ideas before you' he told a cabinet meeting. While there is considerable justification for Lemass's claim, there is nothing to support de Valera's bid to subsume Whitaker's proposals into the 1926 philosophy of Fianna Fáil. De Valera had endorsed the proposals at cabinet as merely a continuation of long-established policy. Many years later he claimed the Whitaker plan differed little from Fianna Fáil policies of 1926. So what was all the fuss about and what did Dr Whitaker's formula contain?

It essentially contained a great deal of straight talking. Whitaker fired from the hip. 'After 35 years of native government', he wrote, 'can it be, they [the Irish people] are asking that economic independence achieved with such sacrifice must wither away?' Professor Oliver MacDonagh said the plan contained, 'Latter-day orthodoxy, a body of Keynesian solutions'. Greater investment by the state in productive industry, an increased role for the Central Bank in directing the commercial banks in how they should invest and the promotion of foreign investment, were all proposed. The First Plan, as the Whitaker Document became known in shorthand, predicted a growth rate of two per cent per annum. Whitaker said 'it was recognised that reliance on a shrinking home market offered no prospect of satisfying Ireland's employment aspirations, and that protectionism, both in agriculture and industry, would have to give way to active competitive participation in a free-trading world'. This new approach, Dr Whitaker said, transformed a spirit of 'disillusionment and despondency into hope and confidence'.

Whitaker warned in his report that 'the greatest fault lies in pursuing a policy after it has proved to be unsuitable or ineffective'. By the time Whitaker had written that warning, Lemass had already arrived at that way of thinking, especially in relation to the protection of native industry. Whitaker may also have been concerned that Lemass might continue his 1955 policy of setting out unreachable job targets and attempting to plan for their creation. Joseph Lee notes that 'it may be surmised that Whitaker was concerned at the prospect of an unbridled Lemass lashing out in desperation if the civil service could not supply him with the weapons he would demand' to attempt to reach the employment targets. Lee also observed that in the First Programme, Whitaker and Lemass 'managed to present a rather bleak prospect as a glimpse of the promised land. The Programme for Economic Expansion, as its very title indicated, was presented to the public as a calculated wager on growth, not as a purgative exercise, which might, at some uncertain distant date, be followed by recuperation'. To Ryan, Whitaker and Lemass in partnership, must go the credit of moving politicians away from the security blanket of industrial protection towards open competition and a planned economy. That move had a profound effect on the way Lemass exercised his premiership.

The nature of that premiership can best be described in Professor Lee's words:

> It was neither his manner of gaining power, or his manner of holding it, that distinguished him uniquely among Irish prime ministers. It was his manner of using it.

Lemass was 60 when he became Taoiseach. He had been elected to the Dail more than 30 years before that. For 20 of those years he had been a senior ranking minister. He moved and thought like a much younger man, however in his first cabinet he did not rush to surround himself with 'the bright young things', nor did he wish to. A contemporary account in *Round Table* recognised the difficulty Lemass found himself in:

> Mr Lemass's principle and most difficult political task will be to rejuvenate the membership and re-orientate the policy of the Fianna Fáil party. If he can accomplish this almost impossible task without friction and disunion he will probably go far; but his time for doing so is short, for a new generation is waiting to take over.

His time was indeed short. He assumed office in 1959 and left in 1966. In that time he strove to direct government policy towards what he himself believed in. No great heavy-weight personal philosophy attended those beliefs, nor were they occluded in the high-flown language of political rhetoric. His beliefs, rather like his personal life, were uncomplicated. He wished to see Ireland assume her responsibilities in the modern world, away from the provincialism of de Valera's 'dreary Eden'. His position, as Brian Farrell has put it 'involved not a denial but rather a redefinition of idealism; less a rejection than a re-inforcing of traditional political aims'. He had, after all, told the Dail, during the debate on the nomination of his first government, that his personal belief was that 'national progress of any kind depends largely on an upsurge of patriotism...directed towards constructive purposes'. If a political philosophy is to be attributed to him, that in essence was it.

Lemass's succession brought an immediate push on the First Programme and an effort at some reorganisation of government, including the establishment of a Department of Transport and Power and the establishment of several planning bodies like the National Industrial Economic Council and a new economic research institute. Most of his interviews in his early years as Taoiseach repeat much the same message.

There was a new mood in the country, he told a press conference in June 1959, which had developed considerably since the publication of the government's programme for economic expansion. The despondency and pessimism which were widespread, now seemed to be disappearing, he said. The rising tide, with which his name was to become inextricably linked, was beginning to lift at least some of the smaller vessels. He indicated that a trade agreement with Britain was on the cards as were exploratory talks about possible developments in western European trade. Discussions that would lead to the signing of a trade agreement with Britain were under consideration. At that stage, he told the journalists, the situation regarding the talks was 'too fluid' to attempt to forecast what might develop.

In the first year in which the Whitaker plan was in operation the rate of economic progress was almost twice that envisaged by the plan. Lemass said the targets had been deliberately set low because he regarded it as important to appear to understate rather than overstate the country's economic development possibilities, thus avoiding any disputes as to the plan's practicability. The early success of the Programme demonstrated Lemass's belief that a co-ordinated programme for economic expansion was possible under Irish conditions. However, in 1960 he stressed that:

> The Programme was never intended to set limits to the scope of government action to induce economic expansion, and indeed, the stimulants and aid to economic progress announced in the Programme have already been surpassed. All government departments and agencies...are continuously exploring new possibilities.

He told *Hibernia* in September 1960 that the most important and urgent problem facing Ireland was the acceleration of economic expansion. Economic viability, full employment and living standards not significantly different from our European neighbours, were achievable, he said.

A theme which would recur again and again throughout his years as Taoiseach centred on his view that the economic problems which faced the Six Counties (as he still called them at that stage) were similar in origin and character to those which faced the Twenty-Six Counties and would, in time, yield to the same remedies. He suggested that if they were tackled on a nation-wide basis they would be more easily overcome:

> I do not know if that view is acceptable in Belfast, but sooner or later I believe it will be, and then perhaps we will be able to get somewhere.

According to the *Belfast Telegraph* that view was not acceptable there. He spoke to the paper's political correspondent T.M. Roberts in

July 1959 and on 9 July the *Telegraph's* editorial stated:

> To say that the economic problems of both parts of the country are susceptible to the same remedies and will yield more readily to action on a nation-wide basis begs the whole of the question of Northern Ireland's integration with the United Kingdom. That cannot be set aside anymore than the questions of loyalty and religion that are also involved – and involved more deeply than Mr Lemass has chosen to admit....It may be observed that Mr Lemass for all the realism that he is trying to inject into the Republic's economic thinking, still believes in...the fantasy that prosperity must wait on the reunion of Ireland.

In almost every major interview in his first year in office he pushed home the message:

> I am personally convinced that the solution of the partition problem will be greatly facilitated when we have demonstrated, in practical results, the economic advantages of freedom.

Lemass's first significant speech, as Taoiseach, on Partition, was made at Oxford University, when he spoke at the Oxford Union on 15 October 1959. He put the case that the unification of Ireland was in the best interests of both islands. He said the ending of partition would make possible 'a fresh approach to consideration of the place of a reunited Ireland in the scheme of western defence'. To support his argument at Oxford he invoked Asquith's famous remark:

> Ireland is a nation; not two nations, but one nation. There are few cases in history...I myself know none, of a nationality at once so distinct, so persistent, and so assimilative as the Irish.

He even invoked the more unlikely source of Winston Churchill:

> Whatever Ulster's right may be, she cannot stand in the way

of the whole of the rest of Ireland. Half a province cannot impose a permanent veto on the nation. Half a province cannot obstruct forever the reconciliation between the British and the Irish democracies and deny all satisfaction to the united wishes of the British Empire.

He told his audience that the case for political reintegration is founded on the position that Ireland is one nation.

As the *Belfast Telegraph's* editorial indicated the Stormont Government was still a long way away from accepting Lemass's thesis, even when he goaded it for accepting the British 'bread of charity [which] is never very filling' and could hardly be acceptable to 'the men of the North [who] cannot be unattracted by the concept of self-reliance.

When pressed by T.M. Roberts of the *Belfast Telegraph* to comment on Lord Brookeborough's statement that 'we in Northern Ireland accept our constitutional status as final and absolute', Lemass used the same argument he put at Oxford three months later:

Ireland is one country. Any other conception ignores the facts of history and geography. We hope to see that essential unity expressed eventually in political institutions. Why should the fiction that 'Ulster is British' stand in the way of the welfare of its people?

I should be surprised if the people of the Six Counties are so satisfied with their present economic circumstances that they will refuse to look at other possibilities of promoting their prosperity.

He put his view on the position of the Catholic minority thus:

It is a fundamental right of the people of a single country that they should be governed on the basis of political unity; and it is a fundamental right of every local minority that their legitimate interests should be respected and that there should be no economic or social discrimination against them.

On the issue of the *de jure* recognition by the Irish Government of the Constitution of Northern Ireland and the means by which better relations between the two parts of the island could be fostered, Lemass took a strong nationalist line. He said the aim of his government was 'the reunification of the Irish people and the abolition of the memory of their past dissensions'.

> We think of it as the coming together of the members of a family who have been divided by disputes and misunderstandings. We hope it will be realised in that spirit. I have no illusions about the strength of the barriers of prejudice and suspicion which now divide the people, but, given goodwill nothing is impossible.

He said the constant long-term aim of all nationalists must be to win over to 'out viewpoint' an increasing number of those in the Six Counties 'who do not now accept it'.

Presaging his historic meeting with captain Terence O'Neill he said 'There must be many who argue that a solution of the problem is worth seeking and who would welcome a serious effort, founded on goodwill, to seek it'.

When it came to the condition under which Lemass visualised a united Ireland, he said the forms and procedures did not concern him. He said de Valera's proposal of the transfer of Westminster's powers over the Six Counties to an all-Ireland parliament, with the local parliament continuing to exist, appeared to him to 'conform with the realities'. He said the fears of Protestants that in an all-Ireland state they would be subjected to disadvantages because of their religion were 'unfounded' but he recognised that such fears must be met.

The decision of Lemass's administration to drop the use of the term Six Counties, which Unionists considered pejorative, and use in its place Northern Ireland, helped create 'a new look at the old policy of partition' *The Irish Times* commented. The papers also said that the rejection by Lord Brookeborough of Lemass's proposal for a Free Trade Area between North and South sparked off a new discussion in Irish Government circles about the need for such an agreement.

In an interview in the *Guardian* on 13 May 1960, Lemass said the negative attitude to suggestions about co-operation in economic matters shown by the Northern Ireland Government was not shared by many Ulster businessmen. Lemass gave an overview of the type of Ireland of which he was Prime Minister:

> We pride ourselves on being a progressive, enterprising people, concerned mainly with the future, busily engaged in building up our economy, developing agricultural and industrial production and exports, and providing jobs to keep our young men and women at home. We are not content with our progress up to date; we are doing our very best to promote a vigorous, expanding economy and we are working for this development in a spirit of confidence and self-reliance.

The view from Belfast on how Lemass's government wished to proceed with the Republic's economic advancement, was articulated on 26 January 1961 by the then Finance Minister of Northern Ireland, Captain Terence O'Neill:

> Soon after coming to power Mr Lemass confided in London that what he wanted for Eire was total economic integration with the United Kingdom – without being a member of even the Commonwealth: all the benefits and none of the responsibilities. The imagination boggles at what this would cost the British Treasury. It would certainly be the most expensive return of a prodigal son in recorded history.

More significant was a stinging rebuff from Lord Brookeborough, made the following month, after Lemass had told the *Scotsman* newspaper that there were signs in the North that the people were fed up with Partition:

> The Unionist Government...is and always has been very close to public opinion on this question, and I deny categorically that there has been any change or sign of one....There is no 'partition' issue. This was all settled 40 years ago, and nothing has since occurred to weaken our determination to stay as we are.

Captain O'Neill's remark about Lemass not wishing to rejoin the Commonwealth took on a further significance in April when a row developed between Lemass and Lord Packenham, (later Lord Longford), over a remark the peer made in a letter to the *Observer* in January. He urged Ireland to return to the Commonwealth. He argued that Partition could only be abolished from within the framework of Commonwealth membership. Lemass remarked caustically on the suggestion in the course of an interview with the writer and traveller George Bilainkin:

> This is not a live issue in Irish politics. No party advocates it. If the idea is ever to be considered it will have to come from Britain; the proposal will never come from here. Even if made by Britain it would be considered only in the context of an arrangement which would restore Irish unity. Lord Packenham...is out of touch with Irish political realities, and his suggestion aroused only momentary interest and little comment.

The remark was reported by the Unionist press in Belfast and by some of the British press. In April, Lord Longford (as he had then become) told the Irish Ambassador in London that he was upset by the Taoiseach's remarks. Lemass wrote a gracious letter to Longford regretting that his remark had caused him to be upset. Longford wrote back placing himself at the Taoiseach's disposal and at the service of Ireland whenever required, and all was well again.

If some sections of the British press picked up on many negative aspects of Ireland in the age of Lemass, others were keen to present the more positive. Norman St John-Stevas, writing in the *Catholic Herald* on 24 June 1960 noted that 'the lost causes are dropped' and 'Ireland is catching up with the twentieth century'. He said the symbol of change was 'Mr de Valera's elevation to the presidency, taking with him to the rarefied atmosphere of Phoenix Park, the two national King Charles' heads of the *non possumus* attitude to partition and the crusade for the Irish language'. St John-Stevas painted this portrait of Lemass for his readers:

> Dynamic, go-getting, realistic, he has not Dev's magic appeal, but he is what Ireland needs, a hard-headed tycoon rather than a romantic visionary. The wind of change is now blowing across the border and chilling for the first time since 1922, the lion-hearts of Stormont. Mr Lemass is making a vigorous and sincere effort to end the border raids, refers publicly to 'Northern Ireland' rather than the pejorative 'six counties,' and has offered full co-operation to the North in all matters of common economic concern.

St John-Stevas was the first British writer to comment favourably on Lemass's handling of the IRA border campaign. 'We aimed to kill it', Lemass said of that campaign, 'by making its futility obvious rather than making martyrs of those who practised it'. Lemass was due to speak in Belfast, at the Queen's University, in January 1961 but the meeting was cancelled after the IRA shot dead a 26 year-old RUC constable, Norman Anderson; he was accused of being a British agent who spied on the families of IRA sympathisers in the Republic. Lemass had, of course, been to Belfast as Minister for Industry and Commerce. He told the South Louth Comhairle Ceantair of Fianna Fáil, on 5 February 1961, that the IRA border campaign 'serves only to help and strengthen those whose purpose it is to keep the nation divided by perpetuating the animosities and tensions on which the case for Partition has always rested. He said their campaign had the effect of 'misrepresenting the national purpose'.

The partition question occupied much of Lemass's time as Taoiseach. During the debate on his nomination as Taoiseach, it was said that he never made speeches on partition. When he became Taoiseach he rarely made a general speech without referring to it.

Amongst the many matters which engaged his attention in his early years as Taoiseach was the establishment of the national television service. A national radio service with a distinctive Irish flavour had been in operation since the 1920s. In March 1958 Mr

Justice George Murnaghan was appointed to chair a commission to advise the Government on the establishment of the television service. In 1960 the government decided, after much debate, to establish the service. The cabinet records for the period show that the government was very concerned about the economic feasibility of the service, and also about the impact it might have on Irish life and attitudes.

A letter from Padraig O'Meara, chairman of Conradh na Gaeilge, asked Lemass to give the television franchise to Gael-Linn. He stated that if Gael-Linn did not run the service 'every young man of spirit will feel there is no future in Ireland and will be forced to emigrate'. A letter from the League of Decency to Lemass invoked 'the help of God and his Blessed Mother' on his choice of the initial directors of the television service. Gael-Linn also proposed building a station that would broadcast into the six counties and said Eurovision should be used so that all programmes televised by the Vatican could be broadcast in Ireland. There were other colourful suggestion on how the new TV service might be controlled but in the end Lemass chose to make it a semi-state body   under the control of an Authority established by the Broadcasting Act 1960.

The Minister for Posts & Telegraphs kept a close eye on the new service in the name of the government. The Broadcasting Act made provision to have direct access to the service, when considered necessary, and it proscribed certain illegal organisations from broadcasting. A letter from Lemass to Andreas Ó Muinhneacháin, former President of the Gaelic League, says that Telefís Éireann will not be a political organ of government and contradicts his most famous remark on the organisation. During *Question Time* on 12 October 1966 he said RTE (it became RTE in February 1965) was 'set up by legislation as an instrument of public policy'. Lemass, principally through the Director of the Government Information Bureau, Padraig Ó hAnnrachain, kept a close watch on the fledgling service, but resisted the temptation to make it an arm of government.
He told Ó hAnnrachain:

The importance of getting understanding throughout the Radio Éireann organisation of their role in relation to national policy in the widest sense of the term is becoming increasingly obvious. I think this is principally the responsibility of the Authority itself.

In a confidential memorandum to Lemass dated 5 October 1962, Ó hAnnrachain gave his opinion of three senior staff at Telefís Éireann. He described the producer and Head of Features, Jack White, as 'belonging to what I might describe as the "de Vere White - Gore-Grimes School" and would think of Ireland as a place where those, like himself, who are "liberal" in outlook, must suffer on as best they can'.

The broadcaster Proinsias MacAonghusa was described in the memorandum as 'a slick operator with considerable talent....I do not think there is anything [he] would not exploit to his own advantage'. MacAonghusa ran into difficulty in 1960 with Kevin Boland, when a radio programme he made on Civil Defence was banned by the then Defence Minister.

The last of the broadcasting trio to come under Ó hAnnrachain's scrutiny was the producer Sheila Richards. She could most charitably be described as a 'non-Catholic', he wrote. The Director of the Government Information Bureau objected to the fact that she had been made producer of the series *Recollections* and commented that while in Montrose one day he saw her 'showing very little respect' for a Catholic priest who was being interviewed on the programme. He suggested her replacement with a 'more Catholic producer'.

Mr Ó hAnnrachain expressed surprise that 'such a rare crew' could get 'a toe-hold on TE [Telefís Éireann] in so short a time'. He said their activities were 'menacing and...the root cause of much of the present troubles in TE.'

All three continued to produce and present excellent programmes for the service and there is no evidence to suggest that Lemass took any action based on the memorandum.

The new television service got on the wrong side of Lemass when a news bulletin misrepresented the vote on his nomination as Taoiseach after the 1961 general election. The Director General, E.J. Roth, wrote to apologise and explained how his Dáil staff was under considerable pressure on the day.

One of Lemass's pet hates was the magazine programme *Broadsheet*. He complained to Ó hAnnrachain on 13 September 1962 that the programme was 'uncritical' and he associated it with 'crank projects'. He said a programme which dealt with foreigners buying land in Ireland adopted a 'sympathetic attitude' to the cranks. He told Ó hAnnrachain to talk with the editors and to let him know the result.

He took the same approach to a journalists' strike at the station in 1963. He advised that he favoured the Authority coming to an agreement with the journalists on the basis of Labour Court recommendations rather than have 'outside intervention'.

Lemass took exception to radio advertisements for hotel jobs in London for Irish girls. They were being offered between £7 and £11 per week. He instructed the Minister for Posts & Telegraphs to do something about it:

> I do not think Radio Éireann should accept advertisements of this kind, and you should write to the Authority to express this view. They are a very definite encouragement to emigration, and must be a considerable embarrassment to hotel proprietors and others who already have difficulty in retaining staffs.

The Minister, Michael Hilliard, assured the Taoiseach in reply, that Radio Éireann had undertaken 'not to accept further advertisements which could be held to encourage emigration'.

The modern Irish Diaspora had its origins in the 1840s and by the 1960s was still an issue that engaged a great deal of the time and attention of the Lemass administration.

In 1929 Lemass said 'the emigration habit which has arisen in some areas can be traced to the initial operation of economic factors' and 'being contrary to the most fundamental human traits will be easily broken down following a revival of prosperity'. In 1938 he said the emigration problem is 'primarily one of employment'. Economic Development stated in 1958 that 'the persistence, decade after decade, in war and in peace, of a high level of emigration is at once the greatest challenge facing Ireland and the greatest obstacle to be overcome in the context of industrial expansion'. Lemass returned to the emigration problem throughout his years as Taoiseach as he had done so many times in the past:

> We are not prepared to watch calmly the de-population and impoverishment of our country. We desire political and economic freedom so that we can take action to protect our vital nationality interests. Unless we are prepared to see the scattering of our people over the face of the world and the destruction of our nation, we must take steps to develop here the industries which mean employment for our people in their own country.

Again that was Lemass speaking in 1929. By 1960 he was still calling emigration 'a most disturbing feature of the present Irish situation'. He called for a study into the non-economic factors which influenced the rate of emigration. In his 1955 Clery's speech he had said that 'our standards must approximate to British standards, or our people will go'. Here was a recognition that staying in Ireland did not necessarily mean conforming to de Valera's vision of rural bliss. James Dillon had drawn attention to the importance of the non-economic factors in 1957 when he put forward the then unpopular view that 'economic want' was not the only reason why people left Ireland. Many left, he pointed out, because they sought a different and better life abroad.

In July 1961, Lemass put his position on emigration, which varied little while he was Taoiseach, thus:

> The continuance of a high level of emigration is, without question, the most disturbing feature of the present situation in Ireland. There is both a 'pull' as well as a 'push'

operating, and it is hard to say which is strongest. The 'pull' is generated by full employment conditions in Britain, while the 'push' is the absence, as yet, of a sufficient variety of occupations in Ireland. The main answer to this problem is more intensive industrialisation. I realise that this is a very inadequate analysis of our emigration problem, because historical and social factors are involved, but a sufficiency of employment opportunities in Ireland, both in volume and variety, must in time reduce emigration to very much lower levels than at present. Already there is in this year, because of recent industrial progress, a not inconsiderable falling-off in the volume of emigration compared with preceding post-war years.

During the 1950s nearly 400,00 emigrants left Ireland. Between 1956 and 1961 net emigration per annum was 42,401, the highest rate since the 'black 1880s'. Nearly 70 per cent of male emigrants were agricultural labourers and smallholders, nearly 50 per cent of female emigrants were domestic servants or hotel staff. Between 1956 and 1961, 197,848 went to Britain and 14,155 went to the US and Canada. By the end of the decade the numbers emigrating dropped radically. There was much rhetoric from politicians about the problem but there was also the realisation that an end to emigration or a dramatic reduction in the figures would mean serious problems in the making at home.

No one in 1960s Ireland encapsulated the spirit of the successful returned Irish emigrant better than John F. Kennedy.

'It took 115 years and 6,000 miles, and three generations to make this trip, but I'm, proud to be here', he said as he stood on the quayside at New Ross from which his great-grandfather had left for the United States in 1848. The visit has been much written about and has become part of the legend and myth of 1960s Ireland. It was a morale booster and helped sweep away the remnants of national self-consciousness which Lemass was anxious to be rid of.

The Minister for External Affairs suggested to Kennedy, through the Irish Ambassador to Washington, Dr T.J. Kiernan, that he might use the occasion of his visit 'to suggest to the British that they indicate publicly that they are not opposed to the unity of Ireland'. Kiernan wrote back that Kennedy's reaction was negative. He told Aiken that Kennedy 'makes no secret of his firm attachment to Britain'. Just before he left for Germany and Ireland, Kennedy stressed to Kiernan: 'Is it understood that I am not publicly to refer to partition? The ambassador assured him that that was the case.

Kennedy's historic address to the Oireachtas made no mention of partition but Lemass in a confidential memorandum noted:

> The President inquired if any progress is being made on partition. I explained that, while there is some evidence of a modification of old attitudes, the position is much as it was. I said that I believed this is a question which, in the ultimate, must be settled in Ireland, that any form of international pressure would not alter the basic situation, and what we wanted from the British government was that they would welcome such a situation in Ireland and that there was no British interest in preventing it.

Kennedy told Lemass that 'a Labour government might be more helpful' but Lemass told him that his earlier experience did not support that view.

Lemass sought a British disclaimer on the North in 1963, on the lines he had spoken to Kennedy about, in a statement which showed adherence to his pragmatic republican stance:

> What we would like to see happening now would be a clear statement by British political leaders that there would be no British interest in maintaining partition when Irishmen want to get rid of it.

When Con Cremin, the Irish Ambassador in London, brought that remark to the attention of Sir Duncan Sandys, Commonwealth Relations Secretary he said 'It would be extremely difficult for British Ministers to say anything which might give the impression that they are, as it were, abandoning the people in the North.'

Duncan Sandys met Lemass in Dublin in 1963 for talks which helped pave the way for the Anglo-Irish Trade Agreement which was signed two years later. They also discussed the 'shock' of Britain's failure to gain EEC entry. Sandys told Lemass that the real reason for the breakdown of Britain's application for membership was that 'there could only be one cock' in Europe and therefore there was no room for Britain. He was referring, of course, to de Gaulle, who managed successfully to keep the British out, resulting in Ireland staying out as well. Lemass told Sandys that in view of the EEC development it would be of mutual benefit for Britain and Ireland to extend their trade agreement.

Since 1957 Lemass had taken responsibility for Ireland's relations with the EEC. When he became Taoiseach he continued that responsibility.

Lemass met Macmillan in London on 18 July 1961 for talks which centred chiefly on Common Market entry. At a press conference in the Irish Embassy after the talks he said no substantial modifications of Anglo-Irish Trade would be necessary if both countries joined the Common Market, other than the gradual reduction of tariffs to comply with the Treaty of Rome. He also pointed out that if Ireland and Britain applied for membership they were likely to be given a voice in the settlement of the EEC's Common Agricultural Policy, which had not been worked out at that stage. He stressed that Ireland would help to get modifications or postponements of the full implementation of the Rome Treaty. And if the British did not apply for membership what would Ireland do?

> One cannot attempt to visualise the circumstance which would exist if Britain decided against joining the Common Market. It is also impossible for us to say at this stage whether we would definitely not seek membership in such an event. The position now is that if Britain decides to apply for membership we will apply too.

He outlined, on several occasions, the difficulties Ireland would face in a Common Market without Britain. He said it was the announcement of the British government's decision to begin negotiations which made Ireland's application feasible.

> If Britain should not, for any reason, acquire membership, we would be faced with a situation of very great difficulty...It is obvious that our interest requires the preservation of arrangements with Britain which would facilitate mutual trade, and that whatever course we take must be such as to permit of this.

On BBC Radio's *Ten O'Clock* programme he was asked if Common Market membership would lead to a 'sweeping away of the border between the two parts of Ireland' but he would only say that 'any removal of impediments between the North and the South – any diminution of the impact of the border is of course to be welcomed'. It would be a further step, he said, but it would not go the whole way.

During the 1961 general election campaign Lemass took every opportunity available to discuss Ireland's application and to explain the benefits of membership to a mystified general public. He exhorted his ministers and deputies to do the same.

He predicted that the Community would develop a political character and said Ireland's decision to seek membership was 'a political decision'. The Irish application involved no reservations 'of any sort including defence' Lemass told surprised reporters who asked if Irish neutrality was being thrown away. He defended his position by offering the view that in the division between the free world and Communism 'we are not neutral'. Neutrality could no longer be defined in the way it was 100 years ago so, he said, 'you have got to be on one side or the other'. He was looking to the day when member states would be required to meet obligations greater than those prescribed in the Treaty of Rome, and while Irish neutrality was not up for sale, it would require a new definition in the new Europe.

Before the 1961 general election intervened the government had an opportunity to consider less serious matters. A Dublin businessman offered £1,000 to remove Lord Nelson from his pillar in O'Connell Street and replace him with a statue of St Patrick. There had been attempts to remove Nelson in 1882 and 1891 and from 1931 Dublin Corporation regularly voted to remove the statue. Lemass looked at the file and decided to leave the old warrior where he stood. A Dublin magazine would later feature Lemass and Captain Terence O'Neill as firemen, in a make-up photograph, among the rubble of Nelson's Pillar after it had been blown up in 1966.

There were lengthy government discussions as to whether the Abbey Theatre should be heated by the ESB or by turf in accordance with the government's preference for native fuels. In the end oil was decided upon.

Several private citizens wrote to complain that the Duke of Edinburgh had been allowed to land at Shannon and deploring that a representative from the Department of Foreign Affairs had been sent to greet him. On New Year's Day 1961, another member of the royal family, Princess Margaret, went to stay with her mother-in-law, the Countess of Rosse, at Birr Castle, County Offaly. Lemass was informed of the arrangements for the visit by the British Ambassador to Dublin and it passed off without major incident. However when the princess returned to Birr in 1965 an ESB transformer was blown up at nearby Abbeyleix.

The Taoiseach intervened to defend the export, for slaughter, of Irish horses to France. The British tabloids sensationalised the facts and at a press conference in London Lemass was asked by an irate journalist 'Do you eat men in Ireland' to which he deftly replied 'In fact we cured the British of that habit'.

Lemass called a general election for October 1961. The campaign, apart from the Common Market dimension lacked any punch. The major international issues of the day failed to make any impact at the hustings. Fine Gael called for the abolition of compulsory Irish, a move ridiculed by Fianna Fáil as being in keeping with the party's ascendancy background. All parties faced into the election with new leaders. James Dillon was now leading Fine Gael and Brendan Corish had succeeded Norton in the Labour Leadership. Fianna Fáil won 70 seats, Fine

Gael 47, Labour 16, Clann na Talmhann 2, Clann na Poblachta 1, National Progressive Democrats 2 and Independents 6.

Lemass was 3 seats short of an overall majority but formed a government with the aid of a few Independents. It survived three and a half years despite loosing some votes in the Dáil.

Lemass told Michael Mills of his reluctance to make cabinet changes just for the sake of change. He was happier working with a team that was well known to him and whose vagaries he had worked out.

> I was always reluctant to contemplate change because you get in the habit of working with the same set of people, you know how to handle them, you know how to get results out of them. With newcomers, no matter how well you think you know them, there is always a bit of a problem. I don't think that I, as Taoiseach, could have done what say Macmillan did, sack half of his government in one day and appoint a new lot of ministers in their stead.

In the 1961 cabinet Charles Haughey became Minister for Justice and later replaced Paddy Smith at Agriculture. The new ministry of Transport and Power was given to Erskine Childers. Gerry Bartley was appointed to Defence and another of the new boys, Brian Lenihan, was made part of the team as Minister for Justice in November 1964. Donogh O'Malley and Brian Lenihan were appointed as parliamentary secretaries in 1961 and George Colley in 1964. Lemass now had two future Taoisigh and a future President in his cabinet. MacEntee, Ryan and Aiken were the last of the party elders in senior ministerial posts and only Aiken would survive the 1965 general election.

Lemass introduced a new style into the relations between Taoiseach and ministers. Brian Farrell writes of the encouragement the new men found from the older man leading their party: ' He not only recruited much younger men to replace his own near contemporaries, he encouraged them to develop their own policy initiatives and their own reputations.' He tended to leave his senior ministers to their own devices but some junior members of cabinet felt the heavy hand of interference from the Taoiseach's office.

Eoin Ryan, a former senator and national executive member of Fianna Fáil and son of Dr Jim Ryan, recalls that in conducting meetings, Lemass was 'very business-like, he tabled an agenda and stuck rigidly to it'. He said in de Valera's day at National Executive meetings something as simple as the resignation of a Cumann chairman could be debated for hours. Lemass, he recalled, would acknowledge the work done by the man, accept the resignation and pass on to the next business. He said Lemass's two great virtues were: 'If he believed a decision had to be taken, he took it, and if after some years he felt that decision had been the wrong one he would willingly admit the mistake and try to rectify it'.

Lemass had exercised considerable patience and self-discipline while standing for so long in de Valera's shadow, or, as *Irish Times* columnist John Healy put it, 'He survived under de Valera and time and again swallowed the bile when the chief had other priorities and insisted on them'. Now that he was in control Lemass was essentially saying, it was time to round up the comely from the crossroads and bus them in to the factories. 'A factory in every town', was, after all, his stated wish. His early interviews with foreign correspondents show that he was anxious to dust down the cobwebs from the icon that de Valera had created. In 1960 he remarked that 'even the BBC television service rarely if ever presents a play about Ireland without the characters moving about in a cloud of alcoholic vapour'.

In January 1962 Ireland joined the Security Council of the United Nations and in April the government announced that Irish exports had reached a record level of £180,300,000 for the year. In July Tyna Mines in County Galway claimed to have struck silver but in fact became one of Europe's biggest suppliers of zinc and lead.

One of the new brand of entrepreneurs encouraged by Lemass, Tony O'Reilly, made major advances with the marketing strategy of Bord Bainne. He travelled over 100,000 miles a year seeking new markets for Irish butter. O'Reilly launched Irish butter under the brand name Kerrygold on world markets, travelling even to Moscow where he recalled his greatest difficulty was not selling butter, but convincing the Russians that he came from Ireland and not Iceland.

On 6 February the government applied for membership of GATT but on the same day Lemass received the bad news that Ireland together with Spain and Greece had been classed as 'under-developed' countries by the Commission on International Trade. Lemass sent a stinging protest to the uncomplaining of what he considered to be a major insult to a country whose economic advance left it well outside the realm of the 'under-developed'.

With discontented farmers simmering and discontented dockers resolving to return to work and containers flowing in and out of Irish ports at hitherto unheard of rates, it could hardly be argued that Lemass was anything but correct in defending the honour of the prosperous Republic against the unfair tag of 'under-developed'.

An Ireland where the work ethic would be respected, was amongst the notions Lemass wished to foster. He faced considerable problems in this regard, many of them visited on his government through industrial unrest. Between 1962 and 1964, there were 217 industrial disputes involving more than 51,000 workers. Ireland remained very near the top of the industrial unrest league table throughout his premiership.

Few doubted Lemass's own extraordinary capacity for work. His routine varied little in his years in political office. He breakfasted in bed where he read all the morning papers. The 'Manager of Ireland Inc' was at his desk by 9.30 a.m., and tried, when possible, to go home for lunch, and by 5.30 p.m. was on his way home again, invariably with a large bundle of files. One minister recalled that 'if you were unlucky enough to engage his attention on some matter at around 5.30, his displeasure would, at times, be barely concealed. On some such occasions he would finish a sentence while moving from desk to door and suddenly he would disappear'. He worked at his papers at home, often into the early morning, when he snatched a few hours sleep before the daily routine began again.

Civil servants who had worked with de Valera in the Taoiseach's office noticed the difference in style. De Valera, like some village headman took a personal interest in the affairs of his immediate civil servants and their families. The Bruree man knew about illnesses, confirmations, bereavements. The Capel Street Huguenot had no time for small talk and his apparently 'gruff exterior' did not invite it. One civil servant noted that his capacity to absorb vast quantities of information quickly, was reflected in the fact that 'documents moved with lightning speed from his IN to his OUT tray'. He did not express a preference for the one page memorandum.

This new style was also evident at the cabinet table. Where de Valera sought cabinet unanimity, often at the price of seemingly endless hours of debate, Lemass sought action. In *Chairman or Chief? The Role of the Taoiseach in Irish Government*, Brian Farrell says Lemass 'recognised that the price of unity could easily become inaction; he believed that a Taoiseach's task was both to hold his team together and to press forward with an active, even controversial, programme'. Lemass usually came to the cabinet table with his mind made up on most major policy matters. While he never stifled debate, his former ministers agree that he had an uncanny sense of when a cabinet discussion had run its course, and at that point he would press the issue. In 1969 he told Michael Mills:

Generally I would agree that the quick decision is always better than the long delayed decision. My own personal experience was that once you had some clear concept of a problem that you rarely added to your wisdom by going back and looking at it again and again and again, delaying the decision. You are just as likely to make mistakes taking the proper decisions as taking the delayed decision, but at any rate you have a decision to work on. As long as you have a certain flexibility of mind you can make adjustments.

This tallies with a light-hearted comment he made in 1953, to the Attorney General, Thomas Teevan (later a Judge of the High Court). He told him that 'the last person the Chairman of the Board of a company should have beside him at a meeting is a lawyer'. He took this attitude with him to the cabinet table. He valued advice but he favoured the quick decision.

Only once during his period as Taoiseach did Lemass have a serious conflict of opinion with one of his ministers. There were differences of opinion but only one came near to a situation of cabinet crisis. The resignation of Paddy Smith as Minister for Agriculture in 1964 should have sent shock waves through the cabinet but Lemass's astute handling of the matter prevented such a situation.

Though a staunch supporter of Lemass for many years, Smith had become a thorn in his side over aspects of agricultural policy. Smith pointed out that the beef industry alone earned more than all industrial exports put together. Lemass obviously knew this but what he sought for Irish agriculture was a development programme which would produce a new race of farmers who were ready to abandon old methods and face the challenge posed by possible Common Market entry. Only three years after Lemass left office did industrial exports exceed agricultural exports. Smith was one of the school who subscribed to the view that Lemass operated an urban bias. Lemass had come to the realisation that he had little chance of convincing Smith that the situation had nothing to do with bias but was, rather, a matter of planning for the future, when agriculture would no longer be the dominant force in the economy. An official of the Department of Agriculture, speaking in the early 1960s, defended the conservatism of Irish farmers in tones which Paddy Smith supported:

Irish farmers are as progressive as we have any right to expect them to be. After all, we spent the last century fighting the landlords, and the first 20 years of this century fighting the British. And we've only just stopped fighting among ourselves.

175

Matters came to a head when Smith claimed that Lemass's excessive show of patience in attempts to settle a two-month long industrial dispute, showed evidence of that bias. In a letter to the *Irish Press,* Smith outlined his objections to the way the unions were, in his view, being given excessive licence. With the delivery of that opinion came the announcement of his decision to resign. Lemass had asked Smith to think it over but by publishing the letter Smith had left Lemass with little option but to accept his resignation. Lemass accepted and moved quickly to replace Smith in Agriculture with Charles Haughey. The news of the resignation of Smith, a Cavan farmer, was overshadowed by the blaze of publicity which attended the announcement of the appointment of a city man to the post of Minister for Agriculture. It was the first time a Fianna Fáil minister resigned over a policy difference with his Taoiseach. What could have been a disaster for Lemass was averted. Luck was on his side. The Dáil was in recess and when it resumed the most notable political fallout from the Smith resignation was a demand from the leader of the Labour Party, Brendan Corish, for the former Minister for Agriculture to withdraw his attack on the trade unions.

The cabinet reshuffle brought Brian Lenihan to the Department of Justice and George Colley to the Department of Lands as Parliamentary Secretary with special responsibility for fisheries. In the Dáil James Dillon objected to the fact that both agriculture and fisheries were now in the hands of two city men. One commentator said the only specialist knowledge of the land the new Minister for Agriculture had, was 'conferred on him by the ownership of a hunter'.

Within Fianna Fáil Sean MacEntee rated as *primus inter pares* when it came to the ranks of Lemass's critics. The most notable non parliamentary party member in that category was Dr Con Ward. Ward, a former parliamentary secretary, was dismissed from office over a scandal involving his tax returns. He had been an able parliamentary secretary at the Department of Health and expected support from Lemass when the scandal broke in 1946. That support was not forthcoming and Ward remained bitter towards Lemass. In 1962 Ward was considering returning to politics. He wrote to MacEntee telling his former minister that his candidature was being blocked by Fianna Fáil HQ and saying that he suspected the hand of Lemass was heavy on the whole affair:

> My personal opinion is that the slick methods of which Lemass is now master will bring about his downfall and the Wards will shed no tears if, and when, his unworthy standards bring about his downfall as Taoiseach.

In the 1960s Fianna Fail did not wash its dirty linen in public. Only a handful of people, and none of them outsiders, would have been aware of such tensions within the party. The nearest the party came, in Lemass's time, to the sort of acrimonious tensions which became all too frequent in its later history, was the Smith resignation.

Paddy Smith's resignation came at a time when farmers were airing their grievances in an organised and public manner. The farmers' leader Rickard Deasy later led protest marches to Dublin to draw attention to low prices for agricultural produce and to complain about the amount of Irish agricultural land being bought by foreigners. The government had little option but to weather the storm. The new Minister for Agriculture refused to receive the farmers' leaders. Lemass stood by his minister and said his government would not be bullied by 'a small group of ambitious men'.

Added to Lemass's troubles was the imposition by the new government of Harold Wilson of a 15 per cent levy on imports to Britain. Lemass moved rapidly after the imposition of that levy to ensure that negotiations leading to the signing of a new Anglo-Irish Free Trade Agreement, were expedited. The Agreement was signed in London on 14 December 1965. The pressure on Lemass to draw the negotiations to a successful conclusion is cited by former ministers as a significant contribution to the decline of his health about this time. The negotiations had been given quite a stimulus by one of the most significant meetings of Lemass's premiership.

Lemass's status in London in 1965 was considerably enhanced by his meeting, on 14 January that year, with the Prime Minister of Northern Ireland, Terence O'Neill.

In a curious way the meeting of these two men symbolised the whole bizarre nature of the northern problem. The Prime Minister of Northern Ireland, O'Neill, could trace his ancestors back in direct lineal descent from Hugh O'Neill, Earl of Tyrone, who was descended from Niall of the Nine Hostages, one of the High Kings of Ancient Ireland. Tyrone was once a very great threat to the Crown in Ireland. His descendant, Captain O'Neill, had no hesitation in describing himself as British. The Prime Minister of the Republic, Lemass, was directly descended from French Protestants who settled in Ulster and finally in Dublin and he saw himself as nothing but an undiluted Irish Catholic.

'Mr Lemass continues to brood about the Partition issue,' O'Neill said in 1963. The Prime Minister of Northern Ireland resented such terms as 'the evil of partition' or any reference to Northern Ireland as 'the Six Counties'.

O'Neill acknowledged to former *Irish Times* journalist, Tony Gray, that much of the credit for the meeting with Lemass must go to Kenneth Whitaker. O'Neill and Whitaker were acquainted through meeting at various international conferences, especially meetings of the World Bank. When interviewed by Gray soon after his meeting with Lemass, Captain O'Neill said : 'I told Ken Whitaker that if I ever became prime minister of Northern Ireland, I wanted him to arrange a meeting with Sean Lemass'.

For his part, Lemass expressed the same willingness when O'Neill took office:

I do not think there can be any misunderstanding regarding my willingness to meet the prime minister to discuss practical problems of common interest and methods of co-operation to solve them and I would welcome an indication that Captain O'Neill would be prepared to talk over such matters.

The actual invitation to Belfast was passed on through O'Neill's private secretary Jim Malley who made an informal approach to

Whitaker in Dublin. He asked for an immediate response. Lemass consulted with Aiken, who had certain reservations, but the Taoiseach overruled them and Malley returned to Belfast with a positive reply for Captain O'Neill.

The arrangements for the meeting were shrouded in secrecy. 'A real James Bond type operation', O'Neill called them. Members of Lemass's cabinet differ in their recollection of whether or not he informed the government before he went North. Neil Blaney says Lemass did not discuss the meeting at cabinet but Charles Haughey recalled that Lemass announced the decision but there was no discussion on it. Whatever the circumstances, the extraordinary thing is that news of the visit did not leak. Lemass did not tell his family. Maureen Haughey said the first she heard of it was on the radio as she drove into Dublin. Lemass's own official driver was told on the morning of departure and initially even the destination was not made known. His orders were simply 'prepare for a long drive'. Even the Rev Ian Paisley was taken by surprise. He turned up to protest a day late.

O'Neill said that if word of the visit was leaked 'all the extremists in the north would be lining the avenue out to Stormont.'

In recent years some historians have played down the significance of the Lemass – O'Neill meeting. They fault it for not addressing constitutional and political questions. It seems a particularly unfair criticism to level at the first meeting of its kind which, after all, lasted only 40 minutes and had the odds stacked heavily against its taking place at all. Its value should be judged as much for its potent symbolism as anything else it achieved. The two leaders discussed a range of economic matters and areas of common interest which led to the very tangible result, not only of O'Neill's return visit to Dublin, but to regular contacts between ministers and officials from both administrations. Within a month of the historic meeting Charles Haughey invited his northern counterpart, Harry West to Dublin and in March, West returned to Dublin to address the Council of the National Farmers' Association, thus becoming the first minister from the

Northern Ireland government to speak at a public meeting in the Republic. In April the Minister for Transport and Power, Erskine Childers, announced the establishment of a joint committee on cross-border tourism in Dublin and Belfast.

Lemass had little to lose and everything to gain by his visit to O'Neill. The northern premiere's position was not quite as clear cut. Certain elements of Unionist opinion called for his blood, even though he was at pains to point out that the meeting would not bring a united Ireland any nearer. 'O'Neill was not strong enough in his own back yard and his enemies used the Lemass visit to undermine him', Charles Haughey believes. What it did achieve was a meaningful step in the direction of breaking the mould in which North-South relations had so long been cast, or as Lemass put it when asked for a comment for the press after the meeting, 'Tell them things will never be the same'.

This new 'hands across the border' approach augured well for Lemass as he faced the general election which he called for April. Even when Taoiseach, Lemass never lost sight of matters relating to party electoral strategy and he welcomed contributions from his deputies on how such matters might be improved. He studied submissions in great detail. In December 1963 Lemass received a confidential memorandum from Charles Haughey proposing a strategy which would 'promote Fianna Fail as the centre party with no sectional ties, able to pursue a course across the board'. To achieve this the memorandum suggested Fine Gael 'must be shown to be the right-wing conservative party and must be strongly attacked. Labour must be established as a well-meaning but misguided group without the experience or prudence to provide sound government'. Haughey predicted that 'the new Labour image which is emerging is a major threat to Fianna Fáil in a general election'. Lemass replied on 20 December 1963:

I do not fully agree with the concept of political tactics contained in the Memorandum which you left with me, particularly so far as it concerns Fine Gael. The presentation of Fine Gael as a 'right-wing conservative Party' implies that they have a definite political philosophy – and one which many people would probably consider as respectable. I think this would flatter them. Indeed they would probably be wiser in their own Party interests to take up a logical and consistent conservative position. They might even, in some circumstances, win an Election on it. Their outstanding characteristic is 'irresponsibility'. Their attitude to the Turn-over Tax, their refusal to indicate how the revenue might be replaced if it were repealed, their £1,000 free-of-interest loan to all farmers, and Mr Dillon's personal attitude are all contributing to this image. The fact is that because they are still hoping for another Coalition with Labour they are forced to cover up their real motivations and to abandon the advantage of having an understandable and logical political position. It is this which is contributing most to the impression of irresponsibility which they are now generating. This is the feeling about them that I have found to be most prevalent. As the art of political propaganda is to say what most of the people are thinking, this would seem to be the right line for us. As for the Labour Party, they are still the Party of 'protest', the recipients of the support of all discontented elements. Nobody seriously thinks of them as a Government, and at best they are seen as a useful check on the Government. I agree, however, that it is their political effectiveness and not their aims which should be the subject of our criticism. There is no doubt that our political campaign should be directed almost entirely against Fine Gael, and that an attitude to Labour of 'well-meaning but ineffective' should be maintained. Our political propaganda must, however, always strive to sound the positive note. It may be true that people find it easier to be 'against' rather than 'for', and we must use this attitude as much as possible, but this should not be inconsistent with the maintenance of the image of Fianna Fáil as the Party which is planning for the future, which has definite aims and a known policy, the displacement of which from office would be the prelude to a period of economic recession.

Fianna Fáil won two by-elections in Kildare and Cork in February 1964. At the end of that year Lemass proposed a variation in the way the Dáil was elected. In a letter to the Attorney General, Aindrias Ó Caoimh, he sought advice as to whether or not the proposal was constitutional. He commented that under the electoral system, in each constituency at a general election there is an unused quota of votes. He proposed that the unused votes be transferred to a 'national' constituency which would return 'persons with exceptional qualifications' who might not be able to secure nomination otherwise. He calculated that in the 1961 general election about 177,000 votes (omitting constituencies where the runner-up was an Independent) which were credited to party candidates, were unused, and would under his proposals, be transferred to the 'national constituency' where their division would see the return of ten additional deputies to the Dáil. (See Appendix B). The Attorney General advised Lemass that the scheme would not be constitutional and his office was unable to come up with a modification which would be. Lemass seemed to have the forthcoming general election in mind when he made his proposal.

In March 1965, in a by-election in Mid-Cork, a bid by Flor Crowley to take a seat for Fianna Fáil from Labour's Eileen Desmond, failed on the third count. Lemass wasted no time reading the auspices. The position of his government was untenable. He felt the timing was right for victory. He was anxious to capitalise on the upturn in the economy. A second economic programme scheduled to run to 1970 was in place and with the popularity of his meeting with O'Neill guaranteed to do him no harm, Lemass led his party into the election with the slogan 'Let Lemass lead on'. The memory of some of his more unpopular decisions, like the introduction of a two-and-a-half per cent turn-over tax in 1963, was beginning to fade. On the other hand, the memory of one of his more popular decisions was still fresh in the public mind. The 12 per cent increase in the 1964 national wage agreement was criticised by the opposition as nothing other than a strategy to win votes in the two by-elections. In the government's 1963 White Paper a wage freeze had been recommended and in the 1965 negotiations the employers had suggested an offer of 8 per cent. The seventh round of wage negotiations in 1959 was the first occasion on which workers believed that their right to share in increases in industrial productivity had been recognised. In previous rounds, wage increases were aimed at compensating for increases in the cost of living. In 1965 Lemass justified the 12 per cent increase in terms of weeding out efficient firms from those who were faltering. It was also a reaction to the epidemic of industrial unrest which plagued his years in office. He called the election for 7 April.

On the campaign trail he criticised Fine Gael for failing to offer a viable political alternative to Fianna Fáil. He said Labour wanted to dictate the shape and policy of the next government but he would not lead a 'yo-yo government jerked on a string by Mr Corish'. Corish stressed that Labour would not go into government with the 'conservative' parties. Sean MacEntee, on his last campaign, joked about the 'two-headed giraffe of Fine Gael.' James Dillon, and Lemass were both facing into their last electoral stands. There was considerable debate within Fine Gael about the shape of its new policy which resisted, yet took on board, much of the *Just Society* document prepared by Declan Costello. At its core the document advocated economic planning, price control, government investment in industry and direct taxation, all wrapped in a Christian democratic framework. For the Fine Gael party of 1965 it was all just a little too ambitious and smacked too much of the influence of what Dillon called 'the young men in a hurry'.

When the result was declared on 13 April it was clear that Lemass had not got the overall majority he had sought. Fianna Fail took exactly half the seats in Dáil Éireann. With 72 seats and Independent support, Lemass was able to form his last government. It was hailed as 'the youngest cabinet in Europe'. A new era in Irish politics was born. Lemass and Aiken were now all that remained of 'Dev's old team'. The age of the new team has been dubbed most memorably as the era of the men in the mohair suits. They would enjoy the trappings of power in a conspicuous way hitherto alien to Irish public life. Not only were all vestiges of de Valera's era swept away from Fianna Fáil but other vestiges of the Irish political system were also swept away in the 1965 general election. With it went the minor parties. The National Progressive Democrats had been dissolved, Clann na Poblachta was reduced to one seat, Clann na Talmhan also disappeared and the Independents were reduced from 6 to 2 seats. The prediction in the memorandum sent to Lemass by Charles Haughey a year before the election had come to pass. Labour did extremely well, taking 22 seats, its largest number since June 1927.

Lemass appointed four new men to his last cabinet. The most notable appointment was that of Donogh O'Malley, who as Minister for Education gained his place in the pantheon of Irish politics for the introduction of a scheme of free secondary education which was one of the last landmarks of the Lemass administration. O'Malley made the announcement without the consent of the Minister for Finance, Jack Lynch, who was out of the country. In fact the announcement was made without the approval of the cabinet. He was castigated by several of his colleagues for his unorthodox methods but the surviving members of Lemass's last cabinet say it was clear that he had the backing of the Taoiseach. Proof that O'Malley had an unenviable task ahead of him was available in an OECD report on the state of Irish education. Half the primary schools in the country lacked running water and proper sanitation. Fifty-seven per cent of boys and 49 per cent of girls left school without having completed their primary education.

Lemass had no serious objection to ministers making announcements outside the formal cabinet channels. However he only issued such dispensations to proposals that had been given his imprimatur.

The other new appointees were George Colley, who was nominated first to Education and later to Industry and Commerce; Joe Brennan became Minister for Posts & Telegraphs and Seán Flanagan became Minister for Health when O'Malley moved to Education in 1966. With these appointments and those of five new parliamentary secretaries, the last Lemass administration was in place and the Taoiseach, to the surprise of many, soon turned his attention to finding his successor.

He announced his intention to retire in October 1966. One version of events is that several months before he announced his decision, Lemass drew Jack Lynch aside and told him he wished him to be his successor. The exact date of the laying on of hands has been disputed, as has the fact that the meeting ever took place. Lynch told author of *Jack Lynch: A Biography*, T.P. O'Mahony, that the meeting took place in mid-September in Lemass's office. He said Lemass asked him bluntly if he was interested in becoming Taoiseach and he told him emphatically that he was not. According to Lynch, Lemass seemed to accept his refusal.

'Some weeks later, he called me into his office again', Lynch recalled, 'this time in the company of Charlie Haughey and George Colley, and again he told us that we should be thinking about the future leadership of the party.'

Lynch says he told Lemass at that meeting that he was still not interested in becoming Taoiseach but, he says, he has no recollection of 'the exact response' from George Colley and Charles Haughey but 'they seemed to indicate that they were interested'.

Charles Haughey does not accept that Lynch was told of Lemass's intentions before any other member of the party. 'Lemass set out to tell us all at the same time', he says. He recalled Lemass telling him: 'I now know that I should go but I cannot guarantee that in five years' time I should have the same detachment about my decision to retire'.

Jack Lynch's reputation for being a reluctant politician may have clouded his recollection of the exact sequence of events for the succession race in Fianna Fáil. He certainly regretted declaring himself to be a 'compromise candidate' after his election as Taoiseach. Frank Aiken, the Tánaiste and Minister for External Affairs, only heard of Lemass's decision in late October. A letter to Lemass from Aiken, who was in New York for a meeting, expressed 'distress' at hearing that he was 'contemplating resignation'. The letter was dated 30 October and Aiken makes it quite clear that he had heard the news second hand from George Colley, who was also in New York on official business. A telegram from Lemass sent Colley hastily home on 'urgent business'. It is clear from Aiken's letter that he discussed the succession stakes with Colley in New York and he advised Lemass thus:

> As I see it George would be the most acceptable to the Party but he could do with another few years' of experience. He would also need time and opportunity to become better known to the country so that he could lead Fianna Fáil to victory in the next election.

Aiken told Lemass that if he resigned it was likely that the government 'would be forced into a general election and it would mean defeat.' He appealed to Lemass to change his mind. 'Both the country and Fianna Fáil need you', he concluded.

Lemass was never close to Aiken, but it seems unlikely that as someone who respected party hierarchy, he would have told Jack Lynch of his intentions to resign before informing the Tánaiste. Aiken's letter supports Charles Haughey's view that Lemass tried to tell the party as a whole that he was resigning. However, as events turned out, his attempts to do so were inadequate and bungled and resulted in sending the parliamentary party into a state of panic. This was very far from his intentions. What he had sought by leaking the story of his imminent retirement to Michael Mills, Political Correspondent of the *Irish Press*, was a breathing space which would allow a successor to emerge. What resulted from that report, despite the fact that the government rushed to deny it, was very much the opposite of what Lemass was seeking.

When Lynch said he was not a contender, Haughey and Colley declared their candidature. They both represented quite distinct factions within Fianna Fáil. Colley was a traditionalist who believed in the sort of core values that would have endeared him to de Valera. Haughey represented the progressive 'young bloods' whose thinking was influenced by Lemass but whose ethos was more brash and assertive. Donogh O'Malley was his campaign manager and nominator but it has been said by party men that when Neil Blaney declared himself a runner, O'Malley's loyalty began to waver. Colley was nominated and managed by Jim Gibbons and backed by the party's old guard. Blaney's campaign manager was Kevin Boland with whom he shared an impeccable Republican pedigree.

When Lemass took over from de Valera, the event had all the hallmarks of an apostolic succession. Now the party was faced with an election for which it had no precedent and which had all the possible elements of a bitter and divisive battle.

To prevent such conflict Lemass again pressed Jack Lynch to let his name go forward. Lynch had greater claim than Colley to the backing of the party's old guard. He had been a deputy since 1948 and a minister since 1957. A group of country deputies also put pressure on Lynch to stand for election. In the end his decision to run seems to have had a great deal more to do with the approval of his wife than pressure from his political peers. Lynch's supporters saw Colley and Haughey as city men who knew little of rural Ireland. They saw Blaney as a 'loose cannon' who was very much a single issue politician. Some of those country deputies, like Martin Corry from Cork and Tom McEllistrim from Kerry made it clear to Lemass that party stability would not be served by the type of contest that was looming.

As soon as Lemass felt confident that that was the general mood in the party he supported the notion of Lynch succeeding him. Blaney and Haughey withdrew. Colley refused and, as little more than token opposition, was beaten by Lynch. The voting was 52 votes to 19.

Jack Lynch later claimed that 'Lemass put his raddle-mark on me' but Lemass's own subsequent reading of the situation contradicts this:

If the Taoiseach begins to indicate whom he wants as successor then, of course, it could be discouraging to a lot of people who felt that they could grow to take the office. This is a very difficult decision to take; to sort of indicate who was going to be the choice of the retiring Taoiseach as successor, because everybody's entitled to feel the office is open to him, providing he works hard enough, providing he's good enough.

There was one other very personal factor which influenced Lemass's decision to retire early. There had been speculation about his deteriorating health even in the mid 1950s. He suffered minor blackouts in 1966 and according to his daughter Peggy, he began to worry about the financial position his wife would find herself in if he should die suddenly. The need to make financial provision for his wife also played an important part in his decision to retire. It allowed him take up several lucrative directorships which, together with his pension, provided a far better basis for that financial security than that offered by his salary from public office.

The private life of Sean F. Lemass has hardly intruded into the later part of this story. A letter of his, to Risteárd Ó Glaisne, who proposed writing a biography in 1961 predicted that this would be the case:

> It has been said that when biographies of a man in public life begin to appear it means that people are beginning to think of him as a 'has been'. I do not wish to put myself, voluntarily, in that category. In any case, I think that my life, if you mean educational attainments and personal experiences, is of minor interest and has little bearing on public events during the past 30 or 40 years.

At the age of 25 when de Valera asked him to become Minister for Defence in the shadow government, Lemass's private life began to yield way to his public career. Kathleen Lemass said she knew this would be the situation from the very first day she married him. There was an unspoken understanding between the couple that 'in moments of national crisis' as Mrs Lemass put it, 'the country would come before the family.' In the first year of their marriage Kathleen Lemass travelled a great deal with her husband. After their daughter Maureen was born she preferred to stay at home.

In an interview in 1975 she recalled that from the very first day Lemass was elected to the Dáil, he asked her to have a suitcase packed and at the ready for him. 'Seán was forever travelling around the country', she recalled, 'trying to build up the Fianna Fáil organisation and during by-elections he hardly slept at all'.

She recalled that de Valera was a frequent visitor to their various homes and as soon as he appeared the children would 'scamper' and he would take up position in 'Dev's chair' for lengthy conferences with her husband. After de Valera was elected president those conferences continued by telephone from Phoenix Park. In the beginning Lemass shrugged them off with good humour but after about a year or so he became quite irritated with de Valera's interference.

Kathleen Lemass said her husband never talked openly about his appointment as Taoiseach but she said she got the impression that 'he had hoped to have the job earlier...Long before he became Taoiseach Dev would consult him on everything, so he appeared to have the power of a Taoiseach except in name.' Most commentators agree that the tragedy of Lemass's career was that he was obliged to await the departure of de Valera, who took what seemed like an eternity to pack the portmanteau containing the vision of his ideal Ireland and remove it to Phoenix Park.

When the Lemass children had married, Kathleen began to travel abroad with her husband on his official trips which included the Vatican, the United States, Canada, Germany, France, Portugal and Nigeria. He insisted that his wife should buy expensive clothes though she often argued with him about that particular expense, on the basis that it was a luxury they could not afford. Sheila recalled her father being 'absolutely furious' when he discovered an unpaid bill from her mother's dressmaker, a Miss McDowell of Palmerston Road. It had been outstanding for three years and when her mother protested that Miss McDowell had not submitted the bill his ire was not quelled and he delivered a lecture about balancing the family budget.

Lemass was extremely fastidious about his own personal appearance. His tailor was F.X. Kelly of Grafton Street and he ordered about a dozen suits a year. He favoured white double-cuffed shirts and in the fashion of the time, plain silk neckties. Lemass and Sean T. O'Kelly were the last two members of de Valera's first cabinet to wear wing collars as late as the mid 1930s. His wife recalled that his tails and dinner jacket had to be ready at a moment's notice. During a visit of Princess Grace of Monaco he told his son Noel that if he did not get his hair cut he would refuse him access to the distinguished visitors. Charles Haughey recalled that he was given a similar instruction from Lemass as the former Taoiseach lay on his death bed.

All three daughters agree that their father never asked them directly if they were in need of money. He would always ask their mother to let him know if they needed financial help. Peggy says their father brought them up to be careful about money and to be self-sufficient. That trait, she says, earned them the sorbiquet 'the uncaring Lemasses.'

Maureen says her father teased them about the need to check their bills because when he was 'on the run' during the Civil War and being housed by a shopkeeper, his food always went on a customer's bill. This was not a sin because 'the customer supported the other side.'

John O'Connor, Lemass's son-in-law, remarked that Lemass had no real sense of the value of money. He recalled an amusing incident after a party Charles and Maureen Haughey gave in their former home, Grangemore, to mark the Lemasses 40th wedding anniversary. While walking in the grounds after dinner, Lemass casually asked his host how much the event had cost him. 'Knowing Lemass's form on money matters', John O'Connor recalls, 'Charlie said it had cost about £200.' Utter incredulity was written all over Lemass's face as he hastily wrote a cheque and disappeared into the distance frantically puffing his pipe. When he was out of earshot Charles Haughey said 'Well it's just as well I didn't tell him that it actually cost me nearly £2000.'

Kathleen Lemass believed that her husband could have made a considerable fortune if he had opted for business instead of politics. He once said that if he had not become a politician he would have opted to live a hermetic life and would have been perfectly happy to spend his days working out complex mathematical problems.

Lemass was cautious in the extreme about being accused of nepotism. It was partly a reaction to the constant corruption charges levelled against him by his political opponents but it also had a great deal to do with his own sense of fair play.

It would be interesting to know how John F. Kennedy reacted to the secret briefing on Lemass prepared for him by the CIA for his trip to Ireland. Would the President have been surprised to read on his plane journey to the old country, that the CIA believed Lemass was an inveterate gambler who got his family into financial difficulties? Was Kennedy shocked to read that the CIA also believed that Lemass was a blackmarketeer during the war? Or would the US President have dismissed this information as inaccurate gossip picked up by the US Embassy's mole, as he ordered his informant another gin and tonic in the Shelbourne Hotel? The briefing seemed to have had little influence on Kennedy if we are to judge by the cordial relations struck up by the two leaders.

A cousin of Lemass who returned to Dublin from London in 1961, wrote to the Taoiseach telling him he had 'sown his wild oats' and asking for help to secure a job in the transport business. Lemass wrote back telling him that such vacancies were not usually brought to the Taoiseach's attention!

This treatment of a cousin may appear somewhat cold but Lemass neither intended coldness nor insult, he simply insisted that he was not in the way of providing 'jobs for the boys' be they family or friend. 'Gruff' is the term most often used to describe his manner. He was reputed to have no capacity for small-talk and to lack affinity with country people. Liam Ruane, whose father Tom Ruane was a Fianna Fáil senator for many years, recalls a different Lemass. He knew him from his visits to Ballina, County Mayo, in the 1950s. He said he was surprised most of all with Lemass's capacity to make jokes at his own expense and also surprised when, at lunch, Lemass directed the conversation away from politics to regale them with stories from the racing world which he dearly loved. The public image did not often allow an airing of that side of his complex personality.

When Jack Lynch was established in the Taoiseach's office Lemass slipped quietly into the background. The new generation of political leaders was in place and only Frank Aiken remained as the last vestige of 'Dev's old team'.

He did not take on the mantle of distinguished elder statesman, though had he wished it, that role would not have been denied him. He remained a deputy until 1969 and was active on the All-Party Committee on the Constitution and, when required, on the Council of State. Younger deputies sought him out for advice. Jack Lynch came to his house during the Arms Crisis and was told: 'I can't help you. You are the Taoiseach'.

He lived for just two years after leaving politics. In those years he concentrated on his family and on his business interests. He was Chairman of Cement-Roadstone Holdings, Unidare Ltd., and Irish Security Services Ltd., and director of Ryan's Tourist Holdings, Waterford Glass, United Breweries of Ireland, James H. North Ltd, John D. Carroll Catering Co., Ltd, Ronald Lyon Estates (Ireland) Ltd, Electrical Industries of Ireland, Bateman Catering, MacDonagh and Boland and Wavin Pipes Ltd.

He was taken ill in February 1971 and admitted to the Mater Private Hospital. He never again saw his home. On Tuesday, 11 May, the 'Manager of Ireland, Inc.' died. The tributes from political leaders, government and opposition, at home and abroad, were fullsome as one might expect. The only dissenting voice was that of the Sinn Féin President, Tomas MacGiolla, who found only negative things to say.

Seán Lemass was given the honour of a full state funeral. On the way from the Mater his remains passed many of the sites associated with his revolutionary days, and many of the sites of the new Ireland which he helped to create.

The tributes and the assessments would fill volumes but none of them can compete with the pungent simplicity of John Healy's prose from his Dáil sketch on the day the House paid tribute to Lemass:

...of the men who survived him to pay tribute to his memory formally in the Dáil...none of them came near the essence of the man...they are genuine in their expressions of regret, but there is not in the speeches one sentence you'd carve on a plaque. One understands Lemass was a big man. Lemass is a big man. Lemass will be a bigger man.

If seeking words to carve on a plaque about Seán Lemass, none could be more fitting than those of Joseph Lee:

It was neither his manner of gaining power, or his manner of holding it, that distinguished him uniquely among Irish prime ministers. It was his manner of using it.

Appendix A

One Nation

A speech delivered by An Taoiseach, Mr Sean Lemass, TD, at a meeting of the Oxford Union Society on 15 October, 1959.

I intend to frame my remarks on the assumption that the decision of the Oxford Union Society to arrange a debate on the subject of the reunification of Ireland implies that the problem created by the partitioning of my country is not regarded as one that concerns the Irish people alone. If it were, it would, I believe, be much easier to resolve in the only way in which we want to resolve it – by peaceful agreement. We would, indeed, regard it as a very useful contribution to the solution of the practical problem of ending it if the British Government would say: 'We would like to see it ended by agreement amongst the Irish. There is no British interest in preventing, or desiring to discourage you from seeking agreement.' This has never been said since 1921, when Ireland was divided under an Act of the British Parliament, passed without the support of a single Irish vote, from North or South. I hope I may be able to convince you that it ought to be said now.

Our Concern is with the Future

I have no intention, this evening, of dwelling at length on the history of the present division. Our concern is with the future. Our basic position has been frequently stated, but it has never been given more emphatic expression than in the words of a British statesman, the then Prime Minister, Mr H. H. Asquith, who said: 'Ireland is a nation; not two nations, but one nation. There are few cases in history, and as a student of history in a humble way, I myself know none, of a nationality at once so distinct, so persistent, and so assimilative as the Irish.' And it was Sir Winston Churchill who once said: 'Whatever Ulster's right may be, she cannot stand in the way of the whole of the rest of Ireland. Half a province cannot impose a permanent veto on the nation. Half a province cannot obstruct forever the reconciliation between the British and the Irish democracies and deny all satisfaction to the united wishes of the British Empire.' It is, indeed, the simple truth that Ireland is one nation, in its history, in its geography and in its people, entitled to have its essential unity expressed in its political institutions.

No One Wanted Partition

We do not accept, any more than the then Mr Winston Churchill was prepared to accept, that a minority has the right to vote itself out of a nation on the grounds that it is in disagreement with the majority on a major policy issue. British law purported to give that right to the Irish minority, and they exercised it under the protection of the British Government. While it is not disputed that a very real and difficult problem existed, that particular solution was the worst that could have been adopted. Nobody in Ireland, North or South, regarded it as a good solution. Very few believed that it would prove to be a permanent one. King George V, speaking in Belfast at the opening of the Northern Ireland Parliament in June, 1921, expressed the hope that it would prove no more than 'the prelude of the day in which the Irish people, North and South, under one Parliament or two, as those Parliaments may themselves decide, shall work together in common love for Ireland upon the sure foundation of mutual justice and respect.' Even Lord Craigavon, the first Prime Minister of Northern Ireland, admitted that it could not last. 'In this island,' he said, 'we cannot live always separated from one another. We are too small to be apart or for the border to be there for all time. The change will not be in my time, but it will come.' The fact that Partition – although it has lasted for almost forty years – is still a living issue of profound significance in Ireland, and in the relations between Ireland and Britain, is in itself sufficient proof that it is not a good, nor likely to prove a permanent, arrangement. For a long time, our attitude towards the solution of the Partition problem was influenced by the conviction that it would eventually collapse of its own inherent weakness and artificiality. We hoped that, when the facts were widely known throughout the world, the judgement of world opinion would bring home to the British Government the necessity for reopening the question.

Finding a Practical Solution

I do not mean to suggest that we ever ignored the original, internal Irish problem which provided the pretext for the idea of Partition, but we are now more actively directing our thoughts towards finding a practical solution of that problem which will be generally acceptable in Ireland, in the confidence that, if such a solution emerges, the British Government will not be able to prevent its adoption, even if they should wish to do so. I have no reason to believe that the British Government – and certainly not the majority of the British public – have any such wish. You may ask: 'Why not leave the situation as it is? Whatever emotional appeal the unity of Ireland may have for you, why not accept the fact of Partition, forget its dubious origins and concentrate on the social and economic progress of the rest of the island – the part which is under your own jurisdiction? 'The answer is that nothing is ever settled until it is settled right. With goodwill on both sides, many of the practical disadvantages of Partition, serious though they are, could probably be reduced by *ad hoc* practical arrangements. But the feelings of the Irish people on this issue are deep and abiding – no less so than the feelings of any other people whose territory has been divided. All history teaches that a continuing sense of injustice and of the frustration of a legitimate national aim operate to discourage or divert efforts for national progress in other directions.

Rights of Minority Disregarded

It is, perhaps, necessary to remind a British audience that, when determining the extent of the area to be cut off from the Irish State, the British Government, even though they sought to justify the whole arrangement by reference to the wishes of a local minority, decided to act on the opposite principle. The Irish border was drawn without regard to the wishes of a large local minority within the Six-County area as a whole and even in direct opposition to the wishes of local majorities in two of the Six Counties, in substantial areas of other counties, and in the city of Derry. It was not based on any historical or geographical foundation. Northern Ireland is sometimes called Ulster, but it does not include the whole of the historic province of Ulster, which comprises nine counties. This was because of the very practical reason that, as was expressly admitted, in Ulster as a whole a Partitionist majority could not be maintained. The principle on which the British Government worked in determining the area to be cut off was to include the maximum number of counties, irrespective of the wishes of their inhabitants, over which the Partitionist minority – mainly concentrated in and around Belfast – could by their voting strength be sure of retaining permanent control. That meant bringing under the jurisdiction of the Northern Ireland Parliament wide areas, adjacent to the Border, in which the majority of the inhabitants favoured union with the rest of Ireland. It may not be generally appreciated in Britain – and, because of recent events, it is now necessary to reiterate – that, over more than half of the whole area under the control of the Northern Ireland Parliament, the majority of the residents would vote themselves out of its jurisdiction if they were given the opportunity.

Argument that Cuts Both Ways

There is no argument which could be advanced to justify giving to the Irish Partitionist minority the right to vote themselves out of the Irish State that could not be applied with greater force to allow County Tyrone, County Fermanagh, South Down, South Armagh and Derry City the right to vote themselves in. In saying this, I do not suggest that drawing the Border elsewhere, so as to reduce the size of the area cut off and to include within the Irish State the areas in which the majority of the inhabitants would vote for inclusion, would satisfy our desire, which is for the reunification of the whole of the national territory, nor would it eliminate the economic consequences of Partition. But I want to make it clear that the feelings of the Irish people about the whole Partition situation are aggravated by the manner in which the division of our country was carried out. One of the consequences of the arrangement is the crude system of gerrymandering the electoral areas to which the Partitionists resorted to prevent the Nationalist majorities in the areas I have named from asserting themselves, even in local government matters. The case of Derry City is a notable example. There, the Nationalists outnumber the Partitionists by more than six to four, but they are unable, because of electoral arrangements specially devised for this purpose and notwithstanding their numerical superiority, to elect more than two-fifths of the City Council or to nominate the Mayor. Similar conditions operate in other areas and contribute to petty acts of discrimination, in such matters as housing and employment, which characterise the local administrations there. The Partitionist politicians seem to regard these undemocratic procedures and arrangements as essential to the preservation of their position. Probably they reflect their own inner conviction of the impermanence of the whole situation and their desire to keep its absurdities out of sight for as long as possible, but even they can hardly believe that these arrangements can persist for ever.

No Normal Political Development

This whole situation has, of course, produced, as might have been foreseen, a very unhealthy political atmosphere in the Six-County area. Preoccupation with the continuing issue of preserving the Partition arrangement has stultified all normal political development. It is the only issue in any parliamentary election in that part of the country, and, even in elections to local authorities, it obscures every other issue. There never has been, and perhaps, under these circumstances, never can be, a change of Government in Belfast or even a normal Opposition offering to the electors the possibility of an alternative Government. The prevailing tensions prejudice efforts to promote better neighbourly relations between the different sections of the people there. If this situation could be brought to an end, it would be like a breath of fresh air throughout the Ulster countryside and one of the best things that could happen the people of Northern Ireland, irrespective of their political or religious alignments. In north-eastern Ireland, political alignments very largely – though not quite exclusively – follow religious differences, and this is a very important factor in the situation there. By and large, Catholics are Nationalists and Protestants are Partitionists. The reluctance of the Northern Ireland Protestant to contemplate joining his Catholic fellow-countrymen in an all-Irish State arises primarily from his fear that there may be some foundation for what he has so often been told – that, in such a State, he would suffer disadvantages because of his religion. However groundless those fears may be, they are very intense and a real barrier to reunification, and nobody can hope to understand or solve this problem who does not recognise how deeply rooted they are.

Full Justice Here for Minorities

That they are, in fact, groundless is shown not only by the unequivocal guarantees of religious freedom and against religious discrimination which are contained in the Irish Constitution but also by the often-expressed testimony of Protestant spokesmen in the Twenty-Six Counties to the absence of any such discrimination or any disadvantages so far as they are concerned. One of their leaders, Professor Stanford of Trinity College, Dublin, speaking last month on the occasion of the opening of a new Protestant school in County Kerry, said: 'In this country there is full justice for minorities, and we have good reason to be thankful to be living here where justice prevails.' We recognise, however, that the fears of Northern Ireland Protestants still exist and that it is unlikely that they could be removed by assurances of good intentions alone, no matter how sincere or how authoritatively expressed. An arrangement which would give them effective power to protect themselves, very especially in regard to educational and religious matters, must clearly be an essential part of any ultimate agreement.

Stormont to Keep Present Powers

Arising from this consideration, it has been proposed that the question of Irish reunification could be considered on the basis of an arrangement under which the Parliament and Government of Northern Ireland would continue to function with their present powers, while an all-Ireland Parliament would exercise the powers in relation to that area now exercised at Westminster. This proposal – which of, course, presupposes that there would be adequate safeguards for the ordinary rights of the Nationalist minority in Northern Ireland – seems eminently practical and should effectively dispose of the apprehensions of the Northern Ireland Protestant population about the consequences of reunification which they seem most to fear. What other assurances or safeguards do they require? In this matter we would go very far indeed to meet them. Such an arrangement would also provide, what is certainly desirable, a means of planning and promoting economic and social developments on a nation-wide basis. Ireland is too small a country not to be seriously handicapped in its economic development by its division into two areas separated by a customs barrier. The fact that its progress has fallen behind that of other countries of Western Europe is certainly due in some measure to this cause, and, since Ireland is probably Britain's largest customer, this has its repercussions on British commercial interests also. Expanding prosperity in Ireland must inevitably benefit Britain. Conversely, anything that retards Irish prosperity must be detrimental to Britain as well.

Economic Co-operation is Possible

Some of the economic handicaps of Partition could, no doubt, be minimised, and some perhaps completely removed, by the growth of a practical system of co-operation between the two areas even in advance of any political arrangement. Such co-operation has already been achieved to some extent in particular matters relating to transport, electricity supply and fisheries. I have repeatedly indicated our willingness to extend co-operation of this kind, but what I have said in this regard has not yet met with an encouraging response from the spokesmen of the Northern Ireland Government.

Perhaps this is because they fear that evidence of the practical value of combined action might lead, in time, to a growing recognition, in Northern Ireland, of the artificial nature of the existing political division. I have not disguised my hope that economic co-operation would eventually bring about this result; but, quite apart from any views one may hold about the eventual reunification of Ireland, is it not plain commonsense that the two existing political communities in our small island should seek every opportunity of working together in practical matters for their mutual and common good? Today, the whole trend of world opinion is towards co-operation and combined effort in trade and economic development.

Ready for Trade Talks Forthwith

An arrangement to facilitate an expansion of trade between the two areas would, as matters now stand, require the concurrence of the British Government, which controls the import regime of Northern Ireland. It would, I believe, remove the reluctance in Belfast to think constructively about it if the British Government would indicate their willingness to facilitate such a development. We, for our part, are ready to enter into trade talks forthwith. It would take much too long to spell out, on a sector by sector basis, how the reunification of Ireland, or at least effective economic co-operation between the two parts of the island, would benefit the development of the whole island as well as open new trade prospects for Britain. The assertion that it would do so may be contested, but very few will feel that it is not worthy of detailed examination. Because of the conditions which have prevailed, that examination has never been made.

No Reduction in Social Benefits

It is sometimes advanced as an argument against unity that in Northern Ireland, notwithstanding the many and serious economic and social problems which prevail, the benefits of

British social welfare scales and certain other advantages are enjoyed and that these scales and advantages exceed those now operating in the rest of Ireland. I think I can say that Irish opinion would accept that with reunification there should be some arrangement to ensure that there would be no reduction of the social benefits now enjoyed there.

Incidents used to Divert Attention

An earlier speaker in this debate referred to the occasional incidents of violence which have occurred in recent years near the Border. I do not think they are strictly relevant to the motion before the meeting except, perhaps, because Northern Ministers have been using these incidents to divert attention from the real issue. Our attitude towards these incidents has been frequently stated and should not be in doubt. As a democratically-elected Government, we have the duty of ensuring that national policy is settled in accord with majority public opinion.

The vast majority of the Irish people support the policy of seeking the reunification of the nation along the road of co-operation leading to agreement. We have the obligation of preventing that aim from being thwarted by the misguided activities of small, armed, illegal groups. We wish to see these activities brought to an end, and all the more so because it is clear that their only consequence is to give the Partitionists an excuse for stifling the expression of more reasonable views and to help them to consolidate their monopoly position in the political life of the north-east.

I began these remarks by suggesting that there is no real British interest in preventing, and possibly no British desire to prevent, if it could be brought about by agreement amongst ourselves. I know that some of you will think in terms of defence and, as is usual in that context, assume that the experiences of the last war point to the requirements of the next. In the Second World War, the territory and ports of Northern Ireland were available for defensive measures by Britain and the United States.

I do not know the extent to which our neutrality in the last war was regarded as a real handicap in British Defence arrangements, and I think there has been a great deal of uninformed comment in that regard. As one of those who took part in the negotiations which led to the handing over in 1938 of the fortified Irish ports to Irish control, I know that, at that time, the British Government were advised that their value in the defence of British sea routes was slight and that no serious disadvantage to Britain would result from their transfer. This view may or may not have proved to be correct, but I have no doubt that it was the emphatic opinion expressed at the time in that regard by British defence departments that facilitated the 1938 Agreement for the transfer of the ports.

Ireland and NATO Alliance

While I do not think it has ever been seriously proposed that facilities in Ireland would be essential for European defence in a future war, the question of our adhering to the North Atlantic Treaty has been publicly mentioned from time to time. Our position in that regard has been repeatedly stated. While the Partition situation remains unchanged, Irish public opinion would be very much divided on any proposal for entering into defensive pacts. A matter so momentous for the future of all Ireland should be determined by a Parliament representing all Ireland. This does not mean, however, that there is or can be any question as to our attitude towards the great issues that now divide the world. Our traditions and values are those of western Christian civilisation; and, in any conflict in which that civilisation was threatened, there could not be a moment's doubt as to the side on which our interests and sympathies would lie – nor, indeed, are there any illusions in Ireland as to our fate if, in a conflict between Communist Imperialism and the Western Democracies, the Democracies should be defeated. The removal of Partition would make possible a fresh approach to consideration of the place of a reunited Ireland in the scheme of western defence.

Cardinal D'Alton's Proposal

Attachment to the Crown, even though it is, in the Six Counties, sometimes reduced to the status of a party badge, and a desire to maintain association with the Commonwealth are often stressed as important factors affecting the outlook of the local majority in Northern Ireland. It is a noteworthy fact, however, that when suggestions were made – in March, 1957 – by Cardinal D'Alton, the Archbishop of Armagh, envisaging the possibility of seeking a solution through the association of a united Ireland with the Commonwealth on the same basis as India, such comment as the suggestions evoked from members of the Northern Ireland Government was unfavourable in its trend. I do not disagree with a statement by another speaker in the debate that, at any conference held to negotiate an agreement, it is probable that the question of the relationship between a reunited Ireland and the Commonwealth would be a main item on the agenda.

Our Goal is Unity by Agreement

Our goal is the reunification of Ireland by agreement, and we cannot expect very speedy results. The barriers of fear and suspicion in the minds of the Partitionists are too strong to be demolished quickly. For that reason, our aim is to develop contacts which will tend to build goodwill and to strive for concerted action in particular fields where early practical advantages can be obtained, hoping to proceed step by step to a new situation in which a reappraisal of the whole problem can be undertaken, unhampered by prejudice. We have expressed our willingness to cooperate with Northern Ireland in this way without, on the one hand, concealing our own ultimate hopes or, on the other hand, asking those in control in Northern Ireland to make any immediate concession to our view which is not dictated by the facts of geography or of our respective economic problems. Apart altogether from our political aspirations, we think that this is a policy of good sense and good neighbourliness. It is impossible to believe that there does not exist in the north-east, particularly amongst the new generation which has grown up since Partition was arranged, a large volume of opinion which would welcome that approach. It is my personal conviction that the economic and social defects persisting in both parts of Ireland derive from the same causes and are susceptible to the same remedies and, whether or not these causes and remedies have a very direct connection with political arrangements, the existence of Partition makes it more difficult to take concerted action about them.

British Government's Attitude

It would be of great advantage to Ireland's future, and to the future of relations between Ireland and Britain, if the British Government would encourage progress on these lines. The confused thinking so noticeable in Belfast is in some part due to an assumption that, in resisting all efforts to widen internal Irish contacts, British interests are in some way being served. It would be for the good of the peoples of both islands if the British Government were to make it clear that this assumption is not truc. Indeed, it would be difficult to overstress the magnitude of thc improvement which would take place in the whole situation in Ireland, if the British Government would now reiterate, in 1959, the hope which was expressed by King George V, in 1921, and indicate that they would welcome the advent of the day when the Irish people, North and South, would work together in common love of Ireland upon a foundation of mutual justice

At the beginning of my remarks I restated our basic position as being that Ireland is, by every test, one nation. It is on that essential unity that we found our case for political reintegration. As I have tried briefly to show this would involve not loss but gain to British interests. It is my conviction that, apart from any specific advantage which it would confer the removal of the last remaining cause contention, in the long history of Irish-British relations, – the last obstacle to unreserved friendship between the two peoples – would be welcomed by British public opinion and would enhance Britain's status throughout the world.

APPENDIX B

Proposed electoral changes sent by Lemass to the Attorney General's office in 1964.

1. In addition to the Dáil constituencies at present set up by law on a territorial basis, there should be established a national constituency embracing the whole State.

2. To keep the total membership of Dáil Éireann within the maximum limit prescribed by the Constitution, the number of deputies to be elected from the territorial constituencies should be reduced to permit of deputies, to a maximum number to be determined by law, being elected from the national constituency.

3. Candidates for election from the national constituency would be nominated only by registered political parties, and should be placed in an order of priority determined by these parties. The nomination day for the national constituency would be the same as for territorial constituencies.

4. When the counting of the votes at a General Election is completed in the territorial constituencies, the balance of votes left unutilised to the credit of a party canditate should be transferred to the national constituency and credited to the party of the candidate for whom thay were cast.

5. Candidates nominated for the national constituency by parties should be declared elected to the Dáil in the order determined by the nominating parties according as there are sufficient votes credited to these parties by transfer from the territorial constituencies.

6. As the votes transferred to the national constituencies would be equivalent to the first preference votes and would not be transferrable between the parties, the rules would provide that such number of candidates would be declared elected for the national constituency as the total credited to each party when divided by a quota equal to the number of vacancies for the constituency, would give full quotas, fractions being disregarded. In practice this would mean that the full number of vacancies would not be filled.

7. Casual vacancies in the national constituency would be filled by the direct nomination of the party concerned.

BIBLIOGRAPHY

Andrews, C.S., *Dublin Made Me: An Autobiography*, Vol.I (Mercier Press, Dublin and Cork, 1979).

— *Man of No Property: An Autobiography*, Vol. II(Mercier Press, Dublin and Cork, 1982).

Barry, Tom, *Guerilla Days in Ireland*, (Anvil, Tralee, 1962).

— *The Reality of the Anglo Irish War*, (Anvil, Tralee, 1974).

Barrington, Ruth, *Health, Medicine and Politics in Ireland 1900-1970* (Institute of Public Administration, Dublin, 1987).

Bell, James Bowyer, *The Secret Army: History of the Irish Republican Army 1916-79* (Academy Press, Dublin, 1979).

Bew, Paul and Henry Patterson, *Seán Lemass and the Making of Modern Ireland, 1945-66* (Gill and Macmillan, Dublin, 1982).

Bielenberg, Andy, The Locke Family and the Distillery Indusry in Kilbeggan', *History/Ireland*, Vol. I, No. 2 (Summer 1993), pp. 46-50.

— *Locke's Distillery: A History* (Lilliput Press, Dublin, 1993).

— *Industrial Development and Irish National Identity 1922-1939* (Gill and Macmillan, Dublin, 1992).

Bowman, John, *De Valera and the Ulster Question 1917-73*, (Clarendon Press, Oxford, 1982).

Carroll, Joseph T., *Ireland in the War Years, 1939-45*, (David & Charles, Newton Abbot, and Crane, Russak, New York, 1975).

Caulfield, Max, *The Easter Rebellion*, (Frederick Muller, London, 1964).

Chubb, Basil, *A Source Book of Irish Government*, (Institute of Public Administration, Dublin, 1964).

— *The Government and Politics of Ireland*, (Oxford University Press, 1974).

— *Cabinet Government in Ireland*, (Institute of Public Administration, Dublin, 1974).

de Vere White, Terence, *Kevin O'Higgins* (Methuen, London, 1948).

Duggan, John P., *Neutral Ireland and the Third Reich* (Lilliput Press, Dublin, 1989).

— *Éamon de Valera* (Gill and Macmillan, Dublin, 1980).

— *Charlie: The Political Biography of Charles J. Haughy* (Gill and Macmillan, Dublin, 1987).

Fanning, Ronan, *The Irish Department of Finance 1922-1958* (Institute of Public Administration, Dublin, 1978).

Farrell, Brian, *Chairman or Chief: The Role of Taoiseach in Irish Government* (Gill and Macmillan, Dublin, 1971).

— *Seán Lemass* (Gill and Macmillan, Dublin, 1983).

Fennell, Desmond (ed.), *The Changing Face of Catholic Ireland* (Geoffrey Chapman, London, 1968).

Fisk, Robert, *In Time of War: Ireland, Ulster and the Price of Neutrality 1939-45* (André Deutsch, London, 1983).

FitzGerald, Garret, *Planning in Ireland* (Institute of Public Administration, Dublin, London, 1968).

Fitzpatrick, David, *Politics and Irish Life 1913-21*, (Gill and Macmillan, Dublin, 1977).

— *All in a Life: An Autobiography* (Gill and Macmillan, Dublin, 1992).

Foster, Roy, *Modern Ireland 1600-1972* (Allen Lane, London, 1988).

Gallagher, Michael, *The Irish Labour Party in Transition 1957-82* (Manchester University Press, Manchester, 1982).

Garvin, Thomas, *The Irish Senate* (Institute of Public Administration, Dublin, 1969)

Girvin, Brian, *Between Two Worlds: Politics and Economy in Independent Ireland* (Gill and Macmillan, Dublin, 1989).

Harkness, D.W., *The Restless Dominion: The Irish Free State and the British Commonwealth of nations 1921-1931* (Macmillan, London, 1969).

Harris, Mary, *The Catholic Church and the Foundation of the Northern Irish State 1912-1930*, Cambridge PhD, 1991.

Keating, P., *The Formulation of Irish Foreign Policy* (Institute of Public

Administration, Dublin, 1973).

Kee, Robert, *The Green Flag: A History of Irish Nationalism* (Weidenfeld and Nicolson, London, 1972).

Keogh, Dermot, *The Vatican, the Bishops and Irish Politics 1919-1939* (Cambridge University Press, Cambridge, 1986).

— 'De Valera, the Catholic Church and the "Red Scare" 1931-1932', in JP. O'Carroll and John A. Murphy (eds), *De Valera and His Times* (Cork University Press, Cork, 1983), pp. 134-59.

Lee, JJ., *Ireland 1912-1985: Politics and Society* (Cambridge University Press, Cambridge, 1989).

Lindsay, Patrick, *Memories* (Blackwater Press, Dublin 1992).

Longford, Lord and Thomas P. O'Neill, *Éamon de Valera* (Arrow Books, London, 1970).

Lynch, Patrick, 'The Irish Economy Since the war, 1946-1951' in Kevin B. Nowlan and T, Desmond Williams (eds), *Ireland in the War Years and After* (Gill and Macmillan, Dublin, 1969), pp. 185-200.

Lynch, Patrick and James Meenan (eds), *Essays in Memory of Alexis Fitzgerald* (Gill and Macmillan, Dublin, 1987).

Lyons, FSL., *Ireland since the Famine* (Weidenfeld and Nicolson, London, 1971).

Mac Conghail, Muiris, 'The Creation of RTE and the Impact of Television', in Brian Farrell (ed.), *Communication and Community in Ireland* (Mercier Press, Dublin and Cork, 1984), pp. 64-74.

MacManus, MJ., *Éamon de Valera* (Talbot Press, Dublin, 1945).

McCabe, Ian, *A Diplomatic History of Ireland 1948-1949: the Republic, the Commonwealth and NATO* (Irish Academic Press, Dublin, 1991).

McCartan, Patrick, *With de Valera in America,* (Brentano, New York, 1932).

McCraken, JP., *Representative Government in Ireland*, (Oxford University Press, 1958)

Mair, Peter, *The Changing Irish Party System* (Pinter Publishers, London, 1987).

Manning, Maurice, *The Blueshirts* (Gill and Macmillan, Dublin, 1970).

Mansergh, Nicholas, *The Irish Free State: Its Government and Politics* (Allen and Unwin, London, 1934).

Meenan, James, *The Irish Economy Since 1922* (Liverpool University Press, Liverpool, 1970).

Mills, Michael, 'Seán Lemass: A Profile', *The Irish Press*, 18 February 1969.

— 'Seán Lemass Looks back', *The Irish Press*, 24 January February 1969.

Mitchell and O'Snodaigh, *Irish Political Documents, 1916-49*, (Irish Academic Press, Dublin, 1985).

Moody, TW., *The Ulster Question*, 1603-1973 (Mercier Press, Dublin, 1974).

Moynihan, Maurice (ed.), *Speeches and Statements by Éamon de Valera 1917-1973* (Gill and Macmillan, Dublin, 1980).

Murphy, John A., *Ireland in the Twentieth Century* (Gill and Macmillan, Dublin, 1975).

Nowlan, Kevin B. and T. Desmond Williams, *Ireland in the War Years and After, 1939-51* (Gill and Macmillan, Dublin, 1969).

O'Carroll, JP. and John A. Murphy, *De Valera and his Times* (Cork University Press, Cork, 1983).

O'Halloran, Clare, *Partition and the Limits of Irish Nationalism* (Gill and Macmillan, Dublin, 1987).

O'Hanlon, Thomas J., *The Irish*, (Deutsch, London, 1976).

O'Sullivan, D., The Irish Free State and its Senate (Faber and Faber, London, 1940).

Patterson, Henry, *The Politics of Illusion: Republicanism and Socialism in Modern Ireland* (Hutchinson, London, 1989).

Raymond, RJ., 'De Valera, Lemass and Irish Economic Development: 1933-1948', in JP. O'Carroll and John A. Murphy (eds), *De Valera and his Times* (Cork University Press, Cork, 1983), pp. 55-71.

Sexton, Brendan, *Ireland and the Crown 1922-1936: The Governor Generalship of the Irish Free State* (Irish Academic Press, Dublin, 1989).

Share Bernard, *The Emergency: Neutral Ireland 1939-45* (Gill and Macmillan, Dublin, 1978).

Stewart, ATQ., *The Ulster Crisis*, (Faber, London, 1967).

— *Edward Carson*, Gill's Irish Lives Series, (Gill and Macmillan, Dublin, 1981).

Swift, John, *Age of de Valera*, (Lee & Tuathaig/RTE, Dublin, 1992).

Tobin, Fergal, *The Best of Decades: Ireland in the 1960s* (Gill and Macmillan, Dublin, 1984).

Walsh, Dick, *The Party: Inside Fianna Fáil* (Gill and Macmillan, Dublin, 1986).

Whitaker, TK., *Economic Development*, (Government Publications, Dublin, 1958).

— *Interests*, (Institute of Public Administration, Dublin, 1983).

Whyte, JH., *Church and State in Modern Ireland 1923-1979*, 2nd ed. (Gill and Macmillan, Dublin, 1984).

Williams, T. Desmond, 'From the Treaty to the Civil War', in T. Desmond Williams (ed.), *The Irish Struggle 1916-1926* (Routledge and Kegan Paul, London, 1966), pp. 117-28.

INDEX